Forbidden
Fighting
Techniques
of the Ninja

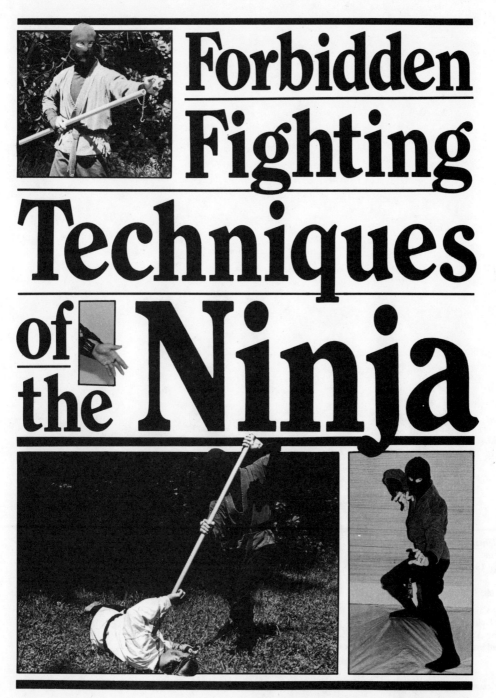

Forbidden Fighting Techniques of the Ninja

Ashida Kim

CITADEL PRESS
SECAUCUS, NEW JERSEY

Forbidden Fighting Techniques of the Ninja
by Ashida Kim
Copyright © 1984 by Ashida Kim

ISBN 0-8065-0957-0

Published by Citadel Press,
a division of Lyle Stuart Inc.
120 Enterprise Ave., Secaucus, N.J. 07094
Manufactured in the United States of America

9 8 7 6 5 4 3 2 1

Direct inquiries and/or orders to the above address.

Photographs by Trish Fredricks-McElroy and Richard Raines.

Contents

INTRODUCTION 1

CHAPTER 1 5
Ninjitsu and Intelligence Gathering

CHAPTER 2 11
Trappings

CHAPTER 3 17
Physical Exercise

CHAPTER 4 27
Stance

CHAPTER 5 35
Defensive Strikes

CHAPTER 6 73
Offensive Strikes

CHAPTER 7 81
Weapons

CHAPTER 8 119
Secret Ceremonies

POSTSCRIPT 122

I dedicate this book to Shendai the Silent—
teacher, friend, father, brother.

Introduction

No one hates war more than the professional soldier.

Gen. Douglas MacArthur

When two old tigers fight, one is killed and one is injured.

Old Chinese Proverb

To affect the lives of men, we must be outside the circle that presses them.

Hsing-i

When my associates approached me a few years ago about publishing a book on ninjitsu, my initial reaction was to take them somewhat lightly. But they persisted, and after many rejections, my work was published by Paladin Press.

Since that time a mania has spread regarding the "silent way" and its disciples. Martial arts were first introduced to America through judo; later one might study karate, after earning a *yudansha* in the gentle way. Then kung fu swept the nation, culminating with the untimely demise of Bruce Lee.

And now it is ninjitsu.

Do not mistake my meaning. Ninjitsu is a fine art. It has enriched my life and been my fortress and defense against enemies both physical and mental. It has performed my will and ruled in all my affairs. In return I have dedicated myself to it.

Our intention in publishing *Secrets of the Ninja* was to preserve some small part of an ancient and obscure art form. Instead we have created a thousand paper dojos and at least a million Ninja masters. Each claims to be the only true messiah of the dark art who will lead you by the hand and make a man of you. They call ninjitsu the "art of winning." It is not! Ninjitsu is the art of *prevailing,* which is not at all the same thing. For one to "win," someone else must "lose." The Ninja is guided by the premise that "he who attacks must conquer, but he who defends need only survive."

Run rather than fight, exhaust every means of escape, cling to neither honor nor glory, and you will not be bound to defend your pride or passion. Revere all life, for each is precious, and none can be replaced.

But if a man's path is such that he leaves you no alternative; if there is no place to run and all the skills of invisibility cannot conceal you; if it is your life which is at stake, then kill without mercy. At that point, your path (which you walk with your own two feet, guided by your own free will) and that of the enemy (which he likewise treads at his own risk) have crossed and it is karma that one of you should die. Never be so foolish as to think that there is a motive that is justifiable in any Heaven you believe to exist that can excuse the taking of a human life.

It has been said around the campfire that killing is an exhilarating experience and one to be envied; this too is a lie. Killing is no more than the swatting of a fly, but can never be undone. Those who relish it have never done it.

My sensei, who preached these principles to me, yet still died in battle, would be ashamed of the mockery that has become known as ninjitsu. A naked man, alone, in an empty room, can practice ninjitsu. It is not the wearing of a mask nor the clanking of a thousand weapons that makes a Ninja. These are merely extensions of the will. It is the state of mind.

Recently, there has been a great deal of emphasis placed on wall climbing ability (chung p'i kung) and masked men clinging to the sides of buildings. Why? Any real Ninja could pass the sentries and enter at will. The costume and the weapons are merely tools of the trade. Use them if need be, collect them if you wish, but do not become dependent on them. When you are disarmed, you will be psychologically vulnerable, and a weapon will not always be handy. Be content to have your hands and feet and a mind which is calm.

Know yourself. If there is any lesson to be learned from study and practice, this is it. Ninjitsu is not for everyone; neither are aikido, tai chi, tae kwon-do, yoga, or mah jhongg. If ninjitsu is for you, I trust you will enjoy the work.

Ninjitsu and Intelligence Gathering 1

There are those who call themselves masters who know nothing of ninjitsu; and there are masters who are totally unaware of their highly developed skills, calling them common sense instead. Most are quiet men, with little regard for the things others might hold dear. They are at peace with themselves and with nature. That they occasionally condescend to teach, or go on some adventure, is most unusual. They train in secret for the most part. This is a tradition from the times when the art was outlawed, as it may be again someday.

One may be hired and trained for one mission, in which case one might be considered expendable. Machiavelli questioned the use of mercenaries in his treatise, *The Prince.* His advice was to avoid them since they "reveled and feasted your lands away in peace and ran in war." As often as not, mercenaries, like the Spartans at Thermopylae, are thrown into battle like so much cannon fodder. They are seldom told the truth about their mission and are frequently killed upon its execution.

On the other hand, one might prove to be a valuable ally, or perhaps even be able to resolve an issue without warfare. Ninjitsu is often a way of achieving the greatest result with the least effort. As Sun Tzu has said, "Sometimes one man in the right place at the right time can change the course of history."

An applicant must be able to document his stated degree in his chosen system, and must be *yudansha* or above. He must demonstrate respect for the sensei, who has sincerely accepted the student. The candidate must also concentrate during training to cultivate patience, and he must practice balance as much as possible.

There are many things which the novice must learn in addition to the techniques of a martial art. First, the dojo is a place of culture, and one must therefore compose oneself and behave seriously both at the time of practice and during a match. One must maintain a good deportment, be attentive to others who are exercising, and by watching them try to learn some helpful lessons in improving oneself.

If one wishes to secure the best results from the practice of the martial arts, one must consistently observe moderation in eating, drinking, and sleeping. One must as a matter of course refrain from eating and drinking water during practice, as well as immediately before and after the exercises. In order to obtain sound sleep, one must always finish everything without danger of being disturbed. Keeping one's body clean and wearing neat costume is necessary for health and out of consideration for others. One should remember to pare one's nails, mend one's costume, and make oneself comfortable before beginning exercises. During the exercises, one should close the mouth and breathe through the nose.

Finally, cooperation should be the ruling spirit to keep the dojo well arranged and to maintain order, since it is the common house of all who use it.

Ta Tso:
Intelligence Gathering—The Work of the Ninja

Know yourself and know the enemy; then you may prevail in one thousand battles.

Sun Tzu, 500 B.C.

The goal of ninjitsu is to become a man of knowledge. To accomplish this, the Ninja are trained in the art of *kuji kiri,* which literally means "nine cuts." This study is divided into nine broad categories, each dealing with an aspect of understanding the nature of man himself. These are: anonymity, discovering the aims of others, gathering intelligence, misdirection, analysis of strengths and weaknesses, counterespionage, self-analysis, manipulation, and understanding of the "universal mind." Each contains aspects of the others, and it is virtually impossible to investigate one without learning something about the others. Because of this type of study, the Ninja often possess great insight and are valued as advisors and agents.

Ideally, training of Ninja agents should be as individualized as possible. In ancient times, the techniques and traditions of each ryu were handed down from father to son in the various families and clans of feudal Japan. Obviously, this allowed a high degree of secrecy, as well as ensuring the loyalty of those instructed. Furthermore, no one would question the authority of the patriarch to decide which skills would be taught, when, and to whom.

During the time of the "sword-hunts" and other periods when teaching the art was forbidden, the clans were often decimated by the forces of law and order. Many schools were totally destroyed, and many families scattered to the four winds. These fragmentary systems frequently died out with those who kept them secret, but some survived as thieves, *yakuza,* or assassins. Others turned their talents to the preservation of peace and harmony in the empire and became agents of the state. Some merely preserved their art for themselves. But the disintegration of the time-honored family system eventually led to the formation of the apprentice method of instruction. Potential agents are referred to specialists for training in a specific skill or for a particular mission. This study is regulated by the student's ability and the sensei's assessment.

In wartime, or when it is necessary to raise an army in the field, it is Ninja philosophy that anyone can learn the principles of the way in a relatively short time. When the demand for agents is great or the need for specialized operational teams arises, it is sometimes necessary to train by classes.

The task, then, is to establish procedures for training spies, saboteurs, and guerrillas. Counterespionage, propaganda, and internal security must be considered, since they are the foundations upon which the lives of the agents and the success of the mission depend. Agent instructors must be able to prepare a wide variety of personnel for the unorthodox activities of the Ninja in the field.

Agents are generally of two types: those who operate in neutral areas on espionage missions, and those who engage in active sabotage and the organization of indigenous guerrilla forces. In practice, however, these are virtually synonymous. The "cover" technique of the spy is essentially the same as that of the saboteur. That is to say, in neutral areas his entry is legal and based upon authentic verifiable documents, while in enemy or enemy-held territory, credentials are frequently forged and entry is gained through infiltration. Consequently, all trainees are provided the same basic information and practice in these areas.

In the field, cover means "to be hidden from the enemy's view but not necessarily from his fire." Cover means the same as "security," and may be equated with the first category of study—anonymity. For the Ninja, there are several types of cover. An agent may be "semi-overt," for example. In a neutral area, he may let it be known that he is a martial artist, thereby attracting other followers of the martial arts to his banner. The actual secrecy of the mission and the methods whereby that mission is to be accomplished, however, must remain inviolate.

Another technique is that used by the infiltrator. In many cases the cover identity is totally false, complete with forged or altered documents. This technique is used primarily for short missions, since the documents will not withstand close scrutiny. An excellent example of this technique is the "beggar pose." The agent disguises himself as a wounded or crippled member of the enemy army, thus passing many checkpoints on sympathy alone. And everyone knows how easily supporting documents may be lost in transit or "misfiled at headquarters."

A variation of this is the partly false cover, in which an individual in a position to execute the mission is replaced by an agent who can adequately fill his shoes. This type of substitution usually requires a period of absence by the replaced individual or a switch in transit.

Cover is basic to all activities of the Ninja; therefore all training stresses the importance of developing and maintaining adequate skill in this field.

In all training, students are forbidden to reveal their real names and must live under assumed identities. Simultaneously, they are encouraged to try to penetrate their fellow students' cover. This creates an atmosphere of tension characteristic of clandestine activities in the field. Students are briefed in the methods of interrogation and are taught the importance of preparing cover down to the smallest detail. This intensive study is designed to prepare the agent psychologically for the constant danger of detection and compromise during his mission.

But to be effective, the agent must take action, even though this makes him more vulnerable. One method of combating this is to use intermediate agents who receive reports from informants and deliver orders from the spymaster. In the event the mission is compromised, the intermediary can flee, leaving the agent to continue with the remaining informants and a new intermediary. Another method is the triad system favored by the Chinese. Each agent within the network knows only one agent above and one below himself. If an operative is captured and tortured into revealing the names of his conspirators, no more than three agents will be lost.

Alternatively, there is the Grand Mute. In this technique, one of the members of the team is designated as the leader. He receives all reports and issues all orders, but he sees each member of the team individually and conceals his identity from them as well. Thus everyone knows he is one of the original group of infiltrators, but no one knows which one. This method requires the establishment of safe houses and a system of safety signals to protect the team. Such recognition signs and sanctuaries also serve as chains or way-stations for incoming and escaping agents.

The study of cover, security, and agent organization are fundamental to the activities of the Ninja. The subjects taught during training are presented as examples of what has been done. Students are discouraged from learning them by rote. On the contrary, Ninja training is designed to sharpen the students' wits, and they are encouraged to expand upon the principles which are taught and exercise their ingenuity and cleverness.

Once the basic toughening and strengthening exercises have been mastered, the students begin to learn the rudiments of intelligence objectives and reporting, escape and evasion, hand-to-hand combat, sabotage, covert entry, and assassination. Each ryu has its own method for teaching most of these, but some techniques are common to more than one style.

Normally, genin are taught anonymity, interrogation, and intelligence gathering; the *chunin,* or middleman, is schooled in misdirection, analysis, and counterintelligence; while the *jonin,* head man, is responsible for the upper levels of investigation and instruction.

Obviously, the best intelligence is gathered by an agent who is actually present. That is to say, if you want to know the number of enemy tanks, you put a man on-site to count them. If you want to know what the enemy general staff is planning, you get an agent in there to observe and report. Unfortunately, even for those highly skilled in the art of invisibility, this is not always feasible. Likewise, with a single agent, transmission of information becomes essential.

Barring direct surveillance, one generally falls back on informants. Probably the best informant is a captured enemy soldier who is terrified of his interrogator. This individual has current data on the field strength of his unit and those surrounding it. By skillful questioning, he can reveal the state of morale and even the quirks of his officers. The prisoner of war does this rarely, being schooled to reveal only name, rank, and service number, and his information is only valuable for a short time, since the longer he is out of contact with his unit, the more changes are likely to occur. If the prisoner can be "turned," however, field intelligence often provides the key to victory.

A similar source is the turncoat, who, for reasons of his own, willingly provides information as an inside source. Such informants may be motivated by jealousy, greed, or even misdirected patriotism. A turncoat can often assist the agent to penetrate the organization being observed, but is also likely to place his own interests before those of the mission.

Another type of inside man is the agent who accepts payment for his services. As has been demonstrated in the past, sometimes this "payment" can be forced on the person to include him in any conspiracy and ensure his silence; or he may simply be recruited. Depending on which appeal is used, his information is normally good and verifiable.

Any raw data must be confirmed by a separate

and independent source. This is not meant to question an agent's loyalty, but rather as insurance that the enemy is not feeding misinformation to an unsuspecting dupe. Analysis is performed by the middle level agents who are guided by the adage, "Don't believe it until you've seen it twice and heard it three times."

When taking an agent's report, the chunin uses his keen knowledge of human nature to skillfully probe for deeper meanings in the information and to discern the enemy's patterns. The field agent, the genin, must also question those who report to him to make sure he has accurately received and recorded the information and to confirm its significance to himself and the informant.

In dealing with outside sources of information, the Ninja should always treat the informant with respect. Bear in mind that he may be acting in fear of his life and can usually stop supplying data at any time. When taking a report, the Ninja should not reveal by word or gesture that any specific item is of value, and occasionally he should ask a question to which he already knows the answer as a verification check. At the conclusion of the report he should express his gratitude for the information and the agent's cooperation. The "control" agent should never make promises he

cannot keep and should always deliver on promises he does make to keep his operatives' faith. Any payment which is due should be promptly made with no chiseling. The Ninja must always act ethically even when others would not; otherwise, they would be no better than the enemy.

The nature of the mission will determine the type of intelligence required. Some is readily available. For instance, check out the newspapers after a robbery or bomb scare. They often describe the means by which the crime was committed with diagrams of how it was done. This information is usually the first released, security is then tightened, and details begin to become hidden or distorted. (Witness the example of "D.B. Cooper.") Remember, the Ninja may be gathering intelligence for a report or for his own purposes. In either case he will want the best available evidence, accurate and up-to-date.

Intelligence gathering relates not only to the clandestine activities of the agent in the field, but also to the collection of information that may be classified as "philosophy." By the act of studying, always learning, and by so doing continuing to grow and better oneself, the Ninja becomes a man of knowledge.

Trappings 2

There are many reasons why one might wish to become a Ninja. A sense of adventure, patriotism, a desire for money. Whatever the motive, it is soon clear to the neophyte that he is entering a world unlike any other.

Even the ancients called espionage the "Great Game." Some modern authors have called the espionage establishment a "circus," and sometimes it is that. At first it is essential to protect oneself at all times, as is advised in the professional fighting arenas. Initially the genin may be more of a liability than an asset. One may do well in tests and simulations and choke under fire; or he may overreact and endanger the entire mission by well-intentioned zeal. Because of this, genin are sometimes relegated to "holding the horses," as it were. One should not be resentful of such an assignment, since no mission can be said to be completely successful until the debriefing of all the agents involved. So the escape is a vital part. Nor should a genin let his guard down, since he is more vulnerable, being stationary, and is usually obligated to defend the escape route rather than flee. Likewise, to most employers, first-timers are generally considered expendable.

Spies, and especially Ninja, have a distinct sense of being apart from others. This is due in part to their enhanced skills and in part to their recognition that each individual must make his own way in the world. Sensei once said that if there were any lessons to be learned from ninjitsu they might be summed up as: "No one can be trusted, nothing is impossible, and nothing can be believed; it is better to tell the truth than lie, better to know than be ignorant, and better to be free than be a slave."

Naturally, one cannot advertise the abilities that make him a valuable agent. Nor can one easily apply for membership in the many covert organizations that exist today. So it falls to the individual to place himself at the scene without outside help. This is good for several reasons. First, one's development of the necessary techniques for arranging transport and passage of equipment will ensure his own security in the field. Second, if the cause is false or fails, there is little likelihood that an employer will be in a position to aid you. On the other hand, you may still provide some service to him if you desire. Third, it is always better to take sides than to try to remain neutral. If the patron is victorious, he is usually generous; if he falls, he will generally try to protect those loyal to him.

In the matter of fees, let it only be said that each man must put his own price on his own life, for that is his wager in the game. A Ninja does not sell himself for a handful of rice.

Shinobi Shozoku:
Ninja Cloak of Darkness

Operations in the field sometimes require the use of special uniforms to aid in the concealment of one's presence. There should be no part of the costume which is distinguished or remarkable in any way. All of the items should be black, nonreflective, and made of soft, unstarched cotton. It must be of a lightweight, portable nature, which can be worn or carried easily; yet flexible enough that a fully clad agent may move rapidly as well as silently. The uniform should be well fitting. Loose or baggy parts are likely to snag; starched or stiff portions rustle. The cloak of darkness is but one of

the weapons of the art of ninjitsu, the Silent Way.
                              Otomo-no-Sanjin
                              Sixth century

With these simple words, the man who was given credit for the victory of Prince Shotoku over Moriya explained his special Ninja night suit. He was awarded the name *Shinobi,* which means "stealer in," in honor of his role as spy, assassin, and saboteur. From this ideogram, the character for "ninjitsu" is derived.

The Ninja's costume is basically that of the stage handler of the kabuki theatre, who sneaks onstage during the scenes to help actors with costume changes, move scenery, or remove props. He is not noticed, even though he may remain in full view for an entire act; he seems a part of the landscape and when he does move, he is so swift and unobtrusive that he escapes notice.

Shinobi shozoku is part of the spiritual heritage of the art of invisibility. It should be worn only when practicing the way. The mask should only be worn during the ceremonies of initiation into the brotherhood. The true Ninja makes no show of force, nor does he display his powers and his abilities lightly to others. A large part of ninjitsu is secrecy. In ancient times, it was forbidden even to speak the name.

The traditional uniform included a hakama (divided skirt for formal wear by men), leggings, sandals, and a light tunic of chain mail. For the contemporary practitioner, the night suit consists of mask, jacket, trousers, gauntlets, tabi, and belt. Each of these is modified to the needs of the modern Ninja.

Ghi Jacket

The Ninja jacket is the single most important piece of equipment the field agent may possess. Like the trousers, it may contain numerous pockets or pouch-like recesses, in which one may hide the items needed for a mission. This model is equipped with a secret patch pocket on the inside of the lapel, suitable for carrying one or more shuriken. Other modifications include two pouch-pockets on the front flap of the jacket below the belt; a deep patch pocket on the innermost lapel; and small flap-type pockets on the shoulders.

In ancient times, the jacket was colored reddish-black or deep blue. This was due as much to the poor quality of the dyes of the period as to a desire

for a black outfit. Any of these shades blend well with the darkness and add to the illusion of invisibility. In combat, the black field of the chest helps to distort the depth perception of the enemy, making the agent appear farther away and smaller than he actually is. When the gauntlets are used, the agent's hands can become completely hidden as they blend into the background of the chest. This not only provides an edge in attacking, but also renders the fingers invisible as they dip into the secret pockets.

The purpose of all this is to enable the practitioner to melt into the shadows, as well as to distort the silhouette. In the technique of *ametori-no-jitsu,* one might fill the jacket with straw to give the enemy a false impression of multiple adversaries or merely to disguise one's true position.

Slip the jacket on as you would any other coat. If you are a man, place the right lapel on the inside and lay the left lapel over it. Women close in the reverse order. The ghi is fitted with two ties on either hip. Attach the tie from the right lapel to the tie on the left hip with a simple square knot. Do not tie it too tightly; part of the ability to vanish depends on discarding the uniform. Anything which hampers the quick removal of the uniform may be significant. Repeat, tying the left lapel to the right hip.

A Ninja would not adorn his uniform with patches or insignia of any kind, as this might be a clue to his true identity or rank. The whole concept of the art is to be unseen. Why then should one wear all these symbols, if not to impress the enemy or himself?

Remember the principle of *mugei-mumei no-jitsu*—"no name, no art." This is the way of the Ninja.

Obi:
The Ninja Sash

One of the most fascinating Ninja weapons was the obi, or sash. In ancient times it was approximately nine feet long. Most often it is worn wrapped around the waist in successive layers with the last end tucked into the circular folds from above. The sash serves admirably as an abdominal support and back brace. As with the blousing ties of the ghi pants, be careful not to wrap too tightly, as breathing is thereby restricted. Be wary of wearing the sash too often or too long, since prolonged use may cause the muscles in the small of the back to atrophy. Instead, think of it as a therapeutic brace, useful if one is injured or if one wishes to add a little support to prevent injury during an assignment. This is analogous to boxers taping their hands, football players their knees, and dancers their feet so that maximum effort may be expended during the performance.

By virtue of its length and because it was usually made of soft cotton, the belt was a valuable climbing tool; since it could act as a rope, it could also be employed to strangle or bind the enemy. The muffling effect when the obi was laid across a gravel path or bed of leaves was significant; likewise, as a bandage the long strip of cloth could bind wounds or serve as a sling or the makings of a litter.

There is a tale told by the goju ryu, who have some links to the ninjitsu tradition, of the magician who was brought out to be executed, clad only in a loincloth. The unfortunate man was so frightened that he trembled and actually urinated on himself. As the escort neared the block, the victim broke away from his captors and sprinted toward a high stone wall. The guards, knowing escape was impossible, did not immediately pursue him. As he ran, the condemned man pulled off the soaked loincloth. When he struck the wall, he slung the wet cloth up to the edge, where, by virtue of its moisture, it clung tenaciously to the stone wall. His momentum carried him a step or two up the surface, and by pulling strongly on the "rope," the Ninja was able to gain the lip of the barricade and swing over it to freedom before the executioners could overtake him. Yet another use of an obi.

Since there are no real belt ranks in ninjitsu, the sash is customarily the same color as the uniform. We have illustrated here the wearing of the obi, spreading the obi across the path, and the obi as a garrote and rope.

Only those of the genin level or above are permitted to wear the obi, since an entire range of medical and military uses are associated with it.

Ninja Gauntlets

The Ninja gauntlets are constructed in a tubular fashion. They are worn as follows: the loop at the pointed end of the cuff is hooked over the second, or middle, finger; the wrist slit is open; the elastic band portion of the cuff is drawn above the elbow; at this time the wrist slit is closed by pressing the two halves of the Velcro closure together.

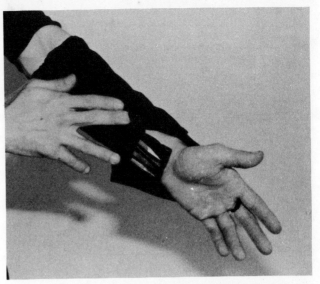

The gauntlet easily conceals any weapon you might place on the forearm, while still keeping it within reach.

Some may wish to adjust this closure to ensure a fairly tight fit about the wrist to prevent snagging. However, one may elect to leave the fit loose so that weapons attached to the wrist and concealed by the cuff may be easily drawn.

Concealment of such weapons as throwing knives or spikes is one function of the gauntlet. In ancient times, they often served to conceal bars of iron or lead, which were sewn into them to act as body armor.

The gauntlets themselves are actually a corruption of the handguards found in kendo. These were designed to protect the back of the hands during *shinai* practice. Ninja often employed these handguards in combat, with or without a sword. Furthermore, it was discovered that when the backs of the hands were covered, it was more difficult to see them against the black background of the ghi jacket. Therefore, almost every ryu has some stance in which the arms are folded across the chest with the fingers turned in to hide the hands.

Ninjitsu is an art based on invisibility, not only of the individuals who practice the style, but also of the fist in combat. Assume a moderately wide horse stance with the left shoulder facing the enemy. Lower your center, form a fist with your right hand, and select the target you wish to strike. Relax, placing the fist on the hara; cover the fist with the left hand. Tuck your chin into your left shoulder for protection, and look the enemy in the eye. Fix his attention. Sweep outward and upward with the left hand; this may be a striking action, as in the backfist, a block, as in a mirror-block or *jodan,* or a palm-up block used to throw sand in the enemy's eyes. Simultaneously step forward with the left foot, closing the gap to the enemy. Kiai! Strike with the fist before the enemy can recover his sight. This is the cornerstone of the hidden hand system.

Hood

It is not the purpose of the hood to conceal the face of the Ninja from others, although it serves that function quite well. It is designed so that the Ninja, by arduous training and study, may divest himself of that part of his personality known as the Ego, and delve instead into the inner sanctums of his mind.

There is a tale of a master Ninja, who, having retired intact, was occasionally asked by the townsfolk for some assistance in their personal affairs. He always insisted that the individual asking the favor go to a secluded spot to discuss the terms of the arrangement in secret. He would then don his mask and sneak up on the petitioner. Using a typical Ninja technique, he would bind the person who had asked for his help, and inform him that his enemy had already come and paid far more money to have vengeance inflicted on the petitioner! Naturally, this led to some negotiation.

By skillfully directing the petitioner to see the error of his vengeful ways, the Ninja mediated disputes in the province for many years, so well that his voice was often sought at council. He usually extracted some penance from those who received this treatment, but excused himself by saying that "only those guilty of the crime of vengeance have made themselves suffer." He was known as "The Priest."

For the contemporary practitioner, the hood may take many sizes and/or shapes. Each ryu has a method of wrapping the obi (sash-belt) around the head to cover the face and sometimes the eyes. This is called MangMuJen Ryu—"Blindman Style" —and stresses techniques performed in total darkness. For our purposes, a simple hood with two eyeholes has been found to be most effective.

The Traditional Scarf Tie

Take a square piece of black cloth, 30 x 30 inches, and cross-fold the corners, making a 48-inch edge. Place the center of this edge against the forehead with the short triangle down the back of the neck. The long ends should be wrapped around the head so they meet at the base of the skull and cross on top of the small triangular piece. Tie a half-knot in the two long ends at the base of the skull. A regular square knot may be used, as it is more secure and larger, but more uncomfortable than any other knot. Tuck the ends of the triangular cloth down the back of the ghi jacket out of sight.

Next, grip one upper corner of the scarf (about 7 x 32 inches) between the tips of the right fingers. Push the corner of the cloth up under the headband with the extended fingers. A fold of the scarf should be placed across the face. Do not do this too tightly, for to do so may interfere with your breathing. Tuck the center of the length of cloth under the headband on the other side.

The traditional two part mask creates a slit for the eyes. The pieces may be discarded after use without suspicion, since alone they do not appear sinister.

Physical Exercise 3

Ninjitsu requires greater physical suppleness than most martial arts. Therefore, the masters devised a series of exercises, each designed to strengthen a specific muscle group or stretch a particular tendon.

Pay particular attention to the section on breakfalls. This art is taught only in the ancient jujitsu system, although the shoulder roll and a few others are known in judo and aikido. The famous Colonel Fairbairn of the Shanghai Police, teacher of the British commandos of World War Two, made the following statement regarding what he termed the "Art of Getting Up": "You will note that no holds or locks on the ground are demonstrated. The reason for this is: THIS IS WAR. Your object is to kill or dispose of your opponent as quickly as possible ... No attempt is made to teach you how to fall, but the following guides are given on how to get back on your feet if you do fall or are thrown." *(Get Tough* by Capt. W. E. Fairbairn, Paladin Press, Boulder, CO)

That was a mistake. If the enemy is properly thrown, he does not get up. The technique of meeting tatami, as the mat surface is known, is one that may often save a Ninja's life. Much of his ability lies in agility and balance. Do not be so foolish as to think that you will never encounter an enemy who can throw you. Even the masters have been thrown; how else could they become masters?

Part of being a Ninja is being strong. There are two kinds of strength: the outer, which enables us to shatter an invincible object with the hand; and the inner, which sustains us throughout life and does not wither with age. Cultivate both, for both are needed.

There have been many definitions of ninjitsu made available to the public by various masters. Some claim that Ninja means "edge man" and the practitioner should keep himself as honed as the edge of his sword. Others say that it is the character for a "sword," held above the character for "heart," thus signifying one who kills with a knife. Then there are those who contend that *nin* means "silent," and *ja* means "agent/man." The earliest texts, however, refer to the "Art which has no name" known as *NienJihTsu,* which means "practice every day." The workout described herein is by no means the complete one available to the Ninja. Each practitioner will discover those techniques which he prefers and will concentrate mostly on those. Every text on physical fitness stresses daily exercise, and the Chinese caution that one should do nothing to excess. Ninjitsu concurs.

Sitting Leg Stretch

Place the sole of the right foot against the inside of the left thigh, and extend the left leg. The palms should be placed on either side of the extended knee. Bend forward, touching the head to the knee. Repeat this procedure by touching the head to the right extended knee ten times. In completing this exercise, extend both legs and bend forward to touch the head to the floor. In addition to stretching the legs, this movement massages the abdomen.

Sitting Leg Stretch Variation

Bring the feet together, placing the palms alongside each knee. Keep the shoulders square.

Next, bend forward from the waist, sliding the palms along the legs. Touch the head to the knees and grip the outside edge of the feet with the hands.

Butterfly Stretch

Place the soles of the feet together and draw them close to the body. This movement may be difficult at first, and tension may be felt in the groin area. The palms should be placed on the extended knees and pressed down slowly and easily. This is a powerful exercise and must be approached with great care. Do ten repetitions of this exercise.

Sit-ups

Used primarily for the development of the abdominal muscles, different types of sit-ups affect different areas of the stomach. The easiest to perform is described below.

Lie supine, feet together, arms at the sides, palms down, and the back straight. Slowly lift the head and then curl the neck and shoulders. Begin to lift the torso off the mat, raising the arms and pointing the fingertips toward the toes. Continue to pull the torso upward, extending the arms until the fingers can touch the toes. Return to the first position and repeat ten to twenty times. Do not swing the arms back over the head when lying back, and do not swing them forward to add momentum to pull you up. To do so defeats the purpose of the exercise.

Sit-up Variation

The following exercise, a favorite of boxers, develops the muscles of the sides of the abdomen as well as those in the center. Interlock the fingers behind the back of the head, and lift the head to look at the feet. Curl the body upward as before. Try not to "pull" with the hands, but use the abdominal muscles instead. As the shoulders become vertical, turn them to first touch the right elbow to the left knee. Next turn the left elbow to touch the right knee. Return to face to the front, and lower once again to the first position. Repeat the exercise, coming up to touch the left elbow first. It is this added "twisting" action that works on the torso.

Push-ups

Stand erect with the feet together. The head should be up, the shoulders back, and the arms hanging easily at the sides. The knees should be straight, but not locked. Lower yourself to the floor, placing the palms face-down on the mat directly below the shoulders. Balance on the hands and toes with the spine straight. Using the strength of the arms alone, lower the body to the floor. Do not rest your weight there, but suspend yourself between your arms. Lift the head, and look straight to the front. This exercise is thus beneficial for the neck. Push up slowly with the arms, lifting the body off the mat. Inhale as you rise, and exhale as you lower your body. Repeat twenty times.

Push-up Variations

Using the same movement as above, perform this exercise while balancing on the fingertips. This serves to increase the strength of the grip and wrist. Perform the push-up while resting the weight on the first two knuckles of the closed fist. This develops the forearms for blocking, strengthens the wrist, and toughens the knuckles for punching.

In doing one-arm push-ups, balance on the palm of one hand, with the feet a shoulder-width apart. This exercise develops the shoulder muscles as well as those of the arm. It is not for the uninitiated. As with some of the other exercises, be careful not to strain too hard at the beginning. Build muscle slowly, and it will last much longer.

Ukemi—Breakfall

Ukemi is the system which enables you to fall safely and easily, avoiding shock or injury from violent impact against the mat whether you fall alone or are thrown by an opponent.

The breakfall is an indispensable and basic technique for the practice of throwing. It is also necessary for proper body conditioning to withstand various strikes and attacks.

Since the art of ukemi engages the entire body, one should start with slow and cautious movements, either lying or squatting close to the mat, and gradually proceed to movements which are made quickly and from a standing position. Finally, one should be able to perform the breakfalls from almost any stance or during any movement.

From the fundamental position, step forward with the left foot, and swing the left arm up above the head.

"Throw" the left arm downward onto the mat so that the elbow is placed near the leading left foot. Tuck the head and push off with the right leg.

Describe a complete circle across the back by letting the left shoulder roll forward so that the right hip will be reached diagonally as you fall.

The weight of the legs coming over finishes the roll. As the right shoulder strikes the mat, the right arm should break the fall by slapping the mat. Simultaneously, the left foot strikes the mat, sole down, to help lessen the impact.

Forward Breakfall

Now that we have learned to roll properly and have diminished our fear of falling, let us turn our attention to the ability to lessen the impact of an unavoidable fall where no roll is possible. In these techniques, the arms serve as shock absorbers and spread the impact over a larger area. Do not try to catch yourself with the hands, as this leads to wrist injuries.

Backfall

From the basic neutral position, prepare for the backfall. This is the most important of the falls in ukemi because it teaches one to "beat" the mat with the arms to break the fall. Timing is very critical in this action. Too early and sprained wrists are likely, too late and the wind will be knocked out of you.

The purpose of the backfall is to prevent injury when the enemy has broken your balance to the rear. It is also used as a "body-toughening" exercise, since a certain amount of impact is bound to occur.

With the feet together, bend the knees quickly and deeply as you swing the arms out in front of the body. Sit straight down. The hips strike the mat first, then the rounded back and shoulders. It is is essential the chin be tucked to prevent banging the head. As the shoulders strike the mat, whip the arms across the body and "slap" the mat. Keep the fingers together, and be sure not to lock the elbows.

Practice this exercise from small heights at first. Gradually train so that you can jump into the air and land. You will then not be injured when meeting tatami.

From a neutral stance, keep the feet apart and the arms at the sides.

Swing the right arm and right leg across the body's midline.

Lower the body on the left leg until the right hip strikes the mat.

Roll onto the right shoulder, slapping the mat with the right hand to break the fall. Begin slowly and progress until you can jump and fall without injury.

Side Fall

The side fall, basic to judo and ninjitsu, may appear quite simple. If one is thrown with a foot sweep or reaping throw, this fall will result.

Establishing the Root

Stand with the feet about two shoulder widths

apart, looking at a spot ten feet in front of you. Compose the mind and regulate the breath. The knees should be slightly flexed and not locked. The arms should hang loosely at the sides, palms resting lightly on the thighs. The tongue should touch the roof of the mouth. Relax.

"Float" the hands up to shoulder level while inhaling. Imagine each hand is suspended by a string at the wrist. The arms rise in response to the wrist being lifted. The wrists droop, allowing the hands to hang as the arms rise. Air, inhaled through the nose, fills the lungs from bottom to top.

Lower the hands to groin level while exhaling, bend the knees, lowering the body, and turn the head to the left. The eyes now look at the horizon. As you exhale, tighten the muscles of the hara (abdominal area), concentrating the chi (life force) in the tan t'ien (a point two inches below the navel.)

Maintaining this position, guide the chi to the heel of the right foot. Since the head is turned to the left, it is impossible to look at the right heel. Therefore, the "I" (mind, thought, attention) must be employed. Holding the tension in the hara, imagine the chi extending down the right thigh, into the knee, down the calf, into the ankle, into the arch of the foot, and finally to the heel, which is slightly lifted off the ground. Hold this pose for five heartbeats.

Raise the hands to waist level, turning the head to face forward once again. Inhale and lift the hands to shoulder level while doing so. Exhale as before, lowering the hands and turning the head to the right. Direct the chi to the left heel and hold for five beats.

Raise and lower the hands a third time, bringing the vision to rest on a spot on the floor ten feet in front of you. At the conclusion of this movement, the hands will be palm down at groin level, the arms relaxed, and the head tipped slightly forward. Dynamic tension will exist in both legs, extending from the hara to the heels of both feet, which are slightly lifted off the ground. The spine will be straight without stiffening, and the shoulders slightly forward.

Inhale, drawing the fists, palm up, to the hips and resting them at waist level. This adds dynamic tension to the upper portion of the body. Lift the eyes and look at the horizon. Maintaining this position, exhale without sound.

Inhale through the nose and expand the abdomen; do not move the chest. Breathe deeply, filling the lower abdomen with your breath. Focus your strength in the lower part of your body and blow the air out through the mouth. Inhale and exhale in a smooth, uninterrupted cycle, avoiding any undue strain. Breathe naturally, always remembering the tan t'ien.

Use the "I" to channel the breath through the body in a definite pattern. When inhaling through the nostrils, picture the air circulating to the back of the head, down the spine and submerging in the tan t'ien before flowing up through the front of the body and out of the mouth. This cycle is used to achieve unification of mind and body.

You must be relaxed, the tongue sticking to the roof of the mouth. If you breathe calmly and slowly, you will feel as though you are actually seeing and hearing your chi circulating throughout the body. This exercise calms the nervous system and strengthens the internal organs as well as curing chronic ailments.

Learning to Stand

It has been said that to learn ninjitsu one must enter a childlike state of wonder. Indeed, the training is designed first to teach one how to move the body by careful exploration; then it moves to the

The "establishing the root" exercise enables you to stand without tipping over. Begin with the right fist loosely clenched, and cover the right hand with the open left hand. In kuji-kiri, this hand position signifies that one possesses secret knowledge.

Top left: Float the hands upward from the hara, fingertips lightly touching. Inhale as you raise the hands (top right), filling the lungs as deeply as possible. Lower the hands to groin level, exhaling as you do so (lower left). Turn the head to the left and then the right on the next inhalation. Turn the head back to the front on the third exhalation (lower right) as indicated in the text.

When the exercise is properly done, the toes virtually grip the floor due to the dynamic tension that has developed. This is the first step in developing the horse stance, which, without this isometric component, is uncomfortable and less effective as a training stance.

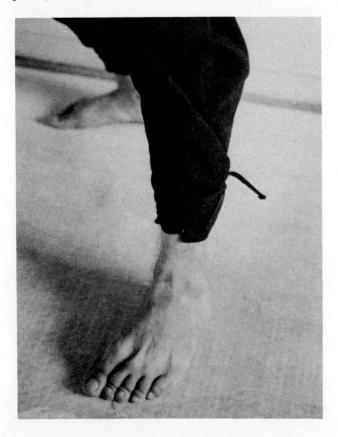

art of falling, at which most infants are adept; and finally it moves to proper standing.

In tai ch'i, this is known as *Wu Lao Chi Shang Chiao*. Wu lao refers to diseases of the five viscera (liver, lungs, heart, kidneys, and spleen), while chi shang deals with the seven diseases caused by failing potency. Since this exercise moves chi along the system of veins and arteries, it is effective in strengthening the internal organs and curing chronic ailments.

You should always maintain a rhythmic flow of breath. Always inhale through the nose and exhale through the mouth. Inhaling through the mouth or holding the breath should be avoided since they cause exhaustion. While exhaling through the mouth, expel the air gradually. It will make you feel as though you are ridding yourself of all the stale air and impurities in your system. Whether you are inhaling or exhaling, you must be constantly aware of an expanding sensation within the tan t'ien.

These rules apply whether standing or moving in a "fist set." After a time, you will discover that your stamina and endurance are greatly increased. This exercise is the basis of the foothold and is known as the horse stance.

Stance 4

Stance is the foundation for any martial art. So it is with the silent way as well. Each of the following positions is a preparatory movement for a specific technique or series of techniques.

Kiba Dachi stresses a powerful base, emphasizes hand techniques, and represents the earth element.

Zenkutsu Dachi is similar to the Western boxer stance. It is symbolic of an impenetrable fortress which can withstand any attack and launch a forceful counter.

Kokutsu Dachi represents the principle of yielding like water to the enemy.

Yoko Dachi, the side stance, enables the practitioner to move quickly from side to side while presenting the smallest and most easily defensible front.

Heng, or cross stance, is the beginning of the poses which enable the Ninja to overcome the enemy without physical contact.

Tsuru Ashi Dachi and *Neko Ashi Dachi* are best used in attacks which rely on kicks as their initial movement. The toe stance is also used to inch forward and steal the march on the enemy.

For withstanding a terrific onslaught or "throwing off a pack of wolves," *Sanchin Dachi* is employed with dynamic tension.

The final stance for this section is *Kasumi Dachi,* which must be learned by all agents, since it is the preparatory step for many of the vanishing techniques characteristic of ninjitsu.

Kiba Dachi:
Horse Riding Stance

Squat slightly and lower your hara, bending the knees forward. This is known as the Horse Riding Stance because it resembles the position of the legs when riding. It is used to strengthen the thighs while practicing blocks and strikes.

Spread the legs by separating the feet two shoulder widths apart. The soles should be parallel to each other and the feet pointing straight ahead. Keep the feet flat on the mat and the knees bent slightly outward. The head, neck, and trunk follow a straight line which pierces the midpoint of the soles. This applies the body weight to the broadest part of the feet. Turn the toes in slightly and grip the floor. The shoulders are back, elbows bent, with the fists palm up on each hip. Center your breathing in the hara and look to the front.

Note: The body is perfectly balanced and upright.

Zenkutsu Dachi:
Forward Leaning Stance

This is the most commonly used stance of many Japanese systems. The feet are one shoulder width apart and the hips and shoulders are square. The weight is distributed 60 percent on the lead leg and 40 percent on the rear. Keep the back straight and bend the forward knee 90 degrees. This produces a low frontal profile (top left). From this stance, the front snap kick is the most effective offensive move, while the lead jab and right cross are the best defensive moves.

Zenkutsu Dachi is used to meet force with force and engage the enemy head-on. It may be used to stalk the enemy by advancing the left leg, then dragging or slide-stepping the right along while keeping the same pose. Such movement is best directed forward. Those who fight from this stance often seek to win with *ikken hiatsu*, or one-punch. Thus they may absorb many attacks while waiting for an opportunity to strike.

In the side view (left), keep the chin tucked and the head down slightly. The shoulders should face the enemy squarely. Hold the fists at the throat and solar plexus levels respectively, with the thumbs on the midline. The elbows remain near

the ribs as a protective measure. The back is straight and the hips aligned with the shoulders. The leading leg is turned in slightly to protect the groin with the lead knee, while the rear leg is essentially straight without being locked. Some practitioners find that lifting the rear heel slightly adds spring to the step and makes it easier to slip the enemy's punches.

Kokutsu Dachi:
Back Stance

While the forward leaning stance places most of the weight on the front leg, the reverse is true of the back stance. Sixty percent of the weight is placed over the rear leg, and 40 percent over the lead leg. This is sometimes referred to as the 4-6 posture (bottom right). The hands are open with the fingertips at throat and solar plexus levels and thumbs on the midline. The shoulders and hips are square (top right).

Movement is accomplished by pulling the left leg. This stance is best employed when retreating before the enemy's advance and is a favorite of counterpunchers. When falling back, the lead leg can be snapped out in a front or side kick, as the hands jab forward along the centerline.

Offensively, in this pose the fighter may seem far away from his opponent, especially if he keeps his guard in close. In reality, the leading foot may be well into the enemy's sphere, where he can be easily reached by a forward shifting of the body.

Kokutsu Dachi is seldom seen as a distinct posture, but often develops during a fight if the enemy is particularly fierce. It is a good stance to practice from for that reason.

Some of the soft systems of China use this fighting pose, together with quick lateral movements, to circle the enemy instead of moving in a straight line.

Yoko Dachi:
Side Stance

Essentially, this is the horse stance from the side. The weight distribution is 50-50 over each foot. The lead hand forms a palm-down, defensive block while the rear hand is placed in the cross chest block position. This stance presents the smallest target to the enemy. One can retreat or advance using the side step. Lateral movement enables one to move quickly out of the line of engagement.

Heng:
Cross Stance

This posture is used to sidestep the enemy and strike from outside the line of engagement. It is considered an advanced pose and is practiced by initiates to develop balance and leg strength. Later it is used to learn directional mobility. Finally, the hidden functions of the stance, which triple its effectiveness, are revealed. The cross stance is sometimes used to circle the enemy and confuse him.

Tsuru Ashi Dachi:
One-Legged Stance

Tsuru Ashi Dachi, sometimes known as the crane stance, may be used as a preparatory position for a strike from ambush; a practice stance for developing balance; or a transitory phase which develops dynamically in combat. All of the weight is placed on one leg, which is held straight without locking the knee. The kicking leg rests lightly against the inside of the platform leg's thigh and the fists are held, one over the other, at the far hip. Do not underestimate the value of this pose. Looking at the horizon when standing on one leg will make it easier to keep your balance.

Neko Ashi Dachi:
Toe Stance

Weight distribution is 80 percent on the rear leg and 20 percent on the lead. This is a favorite of Snake-style fighters. Be careful of quick kicks with the front leg and short steps which enable the user to gradually penetrate your sphere of influence. Unlike the other stances shown, the hips are carried back rather than square. This brings the leading leg just enough into the midline to protect the groin. This stance is excellent for quick, darting movements since one moves on the balls of the feet (tiptoe).

Sanchin Dachi:
Closed Fist Stance

While in this stance, the practitioner can withstand a powerful blow without injury. The muscles of the abdomen form a shield of muscle from the chest to the groin; the hands protect the face; the shoulder blades spread over the back, while the shoulders are rounded and the head is pulled in for safety. The thighs are pressed together with knees facing to protect the groin, and the feet are braced in a toed-in triangular base position for stability. The practitioner attempts to become as small a target as possible and present as much natural body armor to the enemy as he can. This is a pose one might take when completely surrounded or backed against a wall.

Kasumi Dachi:
Vanishing Stance

This is basically a back stance with the arms crossed in front of the chest. The unique feature of this stance is that when the backs of the hands are turned to face the enemy, they become virtually invisible since they are covered by gauntlets. A Ninja can momentarily blind an enemy by bending both knees, making it appear he is moving forward, and aiming the backs of both hands at the enemy's face. He will shift forward to close the gap and flick the fingers of both hands into the eyes of the enemy, then quickly duck out of sight. The entire series of hand gestures used for vanishing from this stance are taught at the chunin level.

Defensive Strikes 5

Blocking movements are seldom what they seem to be in the art of ninjitsu. An observer might mistake the effect of a skillful fighter deflecting his opponent's strikes as a sign of prowess. But there are no blocks in the silent way, only strikes.

In boxing there is a saying, "Make the opponent miss, and make him pay for missing by counterpunching." The Ninja would say, "Break the enemy's arm as he strikes; this will deter further attacks." Counterpunching is a fine art. It is also difficult to learn. Defensive striking, on the other hand, is relatively easy.

Many of the techniques of the Ninja were

The basic back stance is the stance from which the Shan Pi Ta (defensive strikes) shown on this page and the following originate.

Outside middle block

Falling palm block

Palm-up block

adopted so they could be taught quickly to others if need be. Instead of the potential genin having to overcome the fear of being hit in order to get near enough to the enemy to deliver his "trained fist," this system enabled him to remain at fairly long range and humiliate his adversary. Furthermore, it required no risk to the defender, since he never attacked.

Naturally, as the system was refined, the finer points like where to strike on the forearm to numb the hand were added, but these more properly fall into a discussion of wristlocks. The techniques shown here are more than adequate for self-defense.

Philosophically, *shan pi ta* is characteristically Ninja in that the enemy brings about his own downfall by attacking.

Jodan Juji Uke:
Upward Double Cross Block

This upward block is used primarily to protect the head from a downward vertical strike (below). Since it exposes most of the rest of the body to attack, it must only be employed when

the enemy is totally committed to his strike. Its original purpose was to catch a samurai's wrist between the crossed forearms when he attacked with the first cut of kenjitsu. Naturally, range and timing are critical to this technique; too far back and one will catch the blade; too close and the practitioner will break the enemy's elbow. Properly performed, the cross-block can be quickly converted into a top wristlock or an arm twist to disarm the enemy.

From the basic back stance, shift the weight forward over the lead leg, assuming a forward leaning stance to bridge the gap to the enemy, while simultaneously clenching both fists, crossing the forearms just below the wrists, and striking directly upward into the line of engagement. Keep the shoulders and hips square and the back straight. Do not bob up or down when shifting forward, and let the waist (hara) move first.

At close range, *jodan juji uke* may be used offensively to deliver a double reverse hammer fist strike to both sides of the enemy's jaw, or, with the fingers extended, a double reverse sword hand strike to both sides of the throat. The technique would be precisely as described above except that the movement would be preceded by a "Kiai" or "spirit shout" to freeze the enemy. Bring the ribs closer together defensively, and focus the entire energy on the point of impact.

Cross the forearms. Strike upward with a scissors action to strike both sides of the wrist and to trap the hand.

Application of the upper wristlock—Grip the enemy's wrist with your left hand while barring his elbow. Step behind the enemy's leading leg with your left foot. Trip him backwards for the takedown.

The enemy attacks with a vertical sword hand.

Application of the elbow lock—Pull the enemy's wrist downward with your left hand while pushing forward on his elbow with your right hand. To bring him to the mat, step in front of his leading leg with your right foot. He will then trip forward.

Jodan Age Uke:
Rising Forearm

This movement protects the body from waist to head by sweeping that area with the ulnar side of the forearm. In practice, the fist is inverted as it passes the line of the eyebrows to add a snapping action to the strike.

In combat, it may be used simply to take the impact of a blow on the outside edge of the forearm; as an effective shoulder breaker by trapping the enemy's wrist with the rear hand and striking his armpit forcefully from below; or offensively, by shifting forward and striking the enemy's chin from below with an inverted hammer fist.

From the basic back stance, begin by "fading" slightly before the enemy's linear attack to the head or chest to lessen any impact. Bring the rear hand up to guard the solar plexus, and drop the lead hand to waist level.

Shift your weight forward, sweeping upward and outward with the leading forearm.

If your intent is to break the enemy's arm, strike out with a sword hand instead of the hammerfist, as this is faster.

The enemy attacks with a backhand strike to the face or eyes.

Strike your enemy's wrist upward with the right sword hand to break his wrist. Quickly curl your fingers around his arm, pulling him forward.

Strike upward on your enemy's oustretched elbow, thereby breaking the joint.

Shift forward, striking upward on your enemy's armpit. You will thus break his shoulder.

Chudan Soto Uke:
Outside Forearm

This deflection protects the chest area by a circular sweep of the radial side of the forearm. The striking area of the fist is the thumb knuckle, which is braced against the second joint of the index finger.

When striking with the thumb knuckle, one must direct the attack to the more fragile body tissues. While a karateka might deflect an opponent's punch to the outside line with this technique, the Ninja would move in much closer, describe the circular arc with as much speed as possible, and hit the enemy in the temple. The knuckle can easily break through the thin bone and rupture the temporal artery. The concussive effect of this strike alone is sufficient to knock out most men.

From the basic back stance, swing the lead hand back toward the rear elbow, clenching the fist to add power as it arcs upward toward the far shoulder.

Snap the fist across the upper chest in a circular motion to finish the half-circle, and turn the hips slightly to set or brace the action.

This technique is effective against a jab. Let the punch slide past the lead shoulder. This brings the enemy within range. Then strike at his temple or side of the neck before he can pull back.

Face the enemy in a basic back stance as he assumes a right lead stance.

He attacks with a right leading jab. Toe out with your left foot, swing your right arm in a shallow arc in front of the body.

Shift your weight over the lead leg to close the gap between you and your opponent. Strike his temple with the extended thumb knuckle strike.

Strike either the back of his hand or the pressure point on the forearm to open the fist and numb the hand.

Tendan Uke:

Crossing Forearm

This deflection protects the organs of the chest by turning the upper body out of the line of engagement while simultaneously striking across the line with the little finger side of the forearm in a powerful breaking action.

Tendan uke is usually directed at the outstretched elbow of the enemy's jab, and is designed to snap the elbow joint by beating on it with the horizontal hammer fist strike.

Due to the great power generated by the twisting of the hips and shoulders while performing this movement, it is one of the few blocks which can be realistically used against a kicking attack (high roundhouse to head).

From the basic back stance, load the left fist near the left ear as you square the shoulders to the enemy. Fall back slightly in preparation for the enemy's attack.

Whip the forearm laterally in front of the chest in a strong driving motion. Imagine that your arm wields a shield. With this action you bring it up to cover you, as well as striking with the inside edge. This technique, like *chudan,* can be used to hit the nerves of the forearm.

Tendan Uke is very effective when the enemy launches a kicking attack. It is one of the few blocks strong enough to withstand such a strike.

Load the hammerfist near the right ear as the kick begins.

As the kick is extended, trap the leg between your forearms, striking the knee forcefully.

Drop the right hand to catch the enemy behind the knee. Lift with the crook of the left elbow (which effectively traps the ankle), and bear down with the right hand to take the enemy down to the mat.

Gedan Barai:
Downward Block

Gedan protects the groin and the lower third of the body by striking down on the incoming attack and deflecting it to the outside line. It is most often employed against kicks, but may also be used against an uppercut or straight left to the body. When blocking a punch to the leg with the edge of the hand, employ the fist.

The edge of the hand makes the strike faster but less powerful. The hammer fist is stronger, but also slower.

Offensively, when the enemy mounts a strong attack straight down the line of engagement, sidestep and load the fist across the chest. When his momentum brings him down, you are in range to strike the kidney or spine with the same action.

As the enemy attacks, turn slightly away from him and load the left fist near the right ear. Defensively you are covered by the outside of the left arm, the right palm, the left hip, and the outside of the left leg.

Strike down and out in a powerful breaking action to strike the enemy's leg with the shattering hammer fist strike. This works best against a front snap kick but can be used against a low side-kick or roundhouse as well.

The enemy assumes a side stance with his right hand leading.

As he launches his side kick, load the left fist near the right ear.

As the enemy extends his kick, strike down forcefully with the hammerfist. Open the hand at the instant of impact, using the sword hand to break his shin or knee.

Fall back slightly. Raise both hands across your chest as the enemy "chambers" his front snap-kick.

Gedan Juji Uke:
Downward Double Cross Block

This is an extremely powerful double block normally directed at the front snap kick of the enemy. As both hands are used, the upper body is vulnerable to attack. The action may quickly take one of three courses: the enemy may withdraw his leg unharmed and follow through with an attack to the head; the Ninja may use the hands to trap the enemy's leg and throw him to the ground; or the enemy may suffer a broken leg as a result of simultaneous hammer fist strikes to his leg.

From the basic back stance, shift your weight forward over the lead leg to close the gap to the enemy. If he is kicking, you will move toward him rather than away. Make a fist with both hands near the opposite ears and strike down into the line of engagement with a double downward strike.

The fists may be clenched to deliver the strike as shown, or may be opened at the moment of impact to seize the enemy by the ankle or shin. Thereafter, quickly pivot to the inside line while retaining your grip, throwing him to the mat where he may be subdued or finished off.

Shift your weight forward, and execute the "X"-block against the enemy's leg.

Circle the left arm up and under your opponent's ankle to trap his foot. Press down on his calf with your right hand as you turn his leg over.

Drop the enemy to the mat for the coup de grace.

As with other techniques in the Shan Pi Ta system, the first part of the block inflicts pain on the enemy and breaks the momentum of his attack. His attack is turned into a throwing combination by trapping his extended arm or leg.

Wrist Catch:
Hand Trap Block

This technique works best against a straight right to the solar plexus. The lead palm is dropped onto the enemy's wrist, and the hand is gripped by using the small tiger mouth fist; then the entire arm is deflected to one side. Pulling the enemy forward is relatively easy. Remember, "a force of one thousand pounds can be turned by four ounces." The enemy's fist gives him a certain momentum. If his punch is not met with resistance, he will theoretically fall forward.

Once the wrist is seized, a slight tug is usually sufficient to upset the enemy's balance so he may be thrown to the outside line. Alternatively, if the deflection is performed on the inside line, it performs the same function as the knife hand block: to open the enemy's centerline to attack by the rear hand. In this application, one might also chop onto the enemy's forearm.

From the basic back stance, slap downward on the enemy's fist, deflecting it from the line of attack. Open the thumb and curl the fingers to make the tiger mouth. Grab the enemy's wrist.

Pull the enemy's arm down and out to the side.

Face the enemy in the basic stance.

The enemy attacks with a straight left to your body. Fade back in front of the punch in order to widen the gap between you. Defuse the strike as you lift the lead hand with the palm down.

Slap down onto his fist with your lead hand, and seize his wrist using the small tiger mouth fist. Pull down and to the side to jerk him off his feet. The enemy's arm shown here is used to cross the line of engagement. He can also be pulled into a devastating counterattack.

Maintaining pressure on the arm before the enemy can withdraw, shift forward. Snap a backfist strike to his temple to render him senseless.

Gedan Kake Uke:
Low Scooping Block

This technique is best employed against a front kick. By scooping under the leg and lifting, the Ninja can trap the enemy's ankle and throw him by the leg.

From the basic stance, drop the lead shoulder and hand to knee level (above). Shift the weight back, and circle the arm clockwise (top right).

Begin to shift forward, lifting the arms (bottom left).Complete the scooping action and straighten up (below).

The enemy assumes a right lead stance with a high guard.

He then begins to execute a spin-back side kick by pivoting left.

As he chambers his side kick and looks over his left shoulder, begin to drop your left arm in an arc. Your left wrist will then be under your enemy's leg.

Scoop under his ankle, trapping it in the hollow of your left arm. Drop your right palm onto the enemy's heel to complete the hold.

Shift your weight forward, using your grip on the enemy's leg to push him off balance. Begin the takedown.

Pivot on the balls of your feet. Pull strongly toward your right rear corner, pulling your enemy back and down to complete the throw.

Gedan Shuto Uke:
Low Chopping Block

Begin in the basic back stance. As the enemy launches a snap kick or sidekick, fall back over the rear leg in a deep heel stance, lifting the lead toes off the mat for balance. Simultaneously, chop downward on the enemy's leg with the left sword hand. Strike with the intention of "cutting the leg in half," driving the kick to the mat before the enemy can successfully recover. This closes the gap and brings him within striking distance, as well as shattering the tibia.

Having disabled the enemy and prevented him from withdrawing to safety, shift your weight forward once again. Swing the left hand in a circular motion in front of the chest while aiming the back of the wrist at the face of the enemy.

Close the gap between you without stepping, and flick the fingertips into his eyes to temporarily blind him.

In this movement, the leading hand actually makes two strikes, one to the attacking leg and the other to the head.

As the enemy is about to launch a front snap kick, shift slightly backward by pushing with the lead leg and moving the hips. The gap between you and your enemy is thus increased. By its subtle action alone, this movement will often cause the enemy to misjudge the depth of his attack.

As the enemy chambers the kick, lower your lead hand.

When the opponent's kick is thrown, slap down on his knee and catch the ankle. Rock backward.

"Rolling back" with your enemy's leg held as shown will effectively lock his knee and prevent him from further assaulting you. You may strike down with the lead hand to break his knee. (Such a strike requires about forty pounds of force.) To take the enemy down, push straight back against his line of balance.

She Uke:
Serpent Parry

Begin in the fundamental fighting position with the weight slightly back and the hands protecting the centerline. As the enemy attacks with a side-kick, lift the leading elbow and shift to the right as you square the shoulders to the enemy.

As the kick approaches, keep the elbow up and drop the leading palm down onto the enemy's leg.

Cup the fingers as they strike the enemy's leg, catching it by the shin or calf.

This, like the scooping block, is used to trap the kick and throw the enemy by his leg.

Observing that the enemy is chambering his lead leg for a side kick, withdraw slightly to widen the gap between you.

Invert the leading palm and slap the enemy's heel. Grip his foot by the large calcaneus bone (heel) and dig your thumb and fingers into the foot to seize the Achilles tendon.

Pull your enemy's leg toward your hip to lock the knee. Quickly lift up to drop him to the mat.

Shinobi Shou:
Ninja Palm

Since the palm is stronger and more flexible than the fist, it is frequently preferred as a weapon. The Ninja palm exercise illustrates the principles of proper redirection of an attacker's force.

In the first movement, the hand is extended

and raised into the line of engagement to facilitate quick, efficient blocks; the second part is used to pinch the underside of the arm; while the next action carries the incoming punch or kick downward. It is the last turning over of the palm which actually pushes an attack to the side or catches the enemy's wrist.

The rising palm (top left) deflects an attack to either side of the line of engagement, while the lifting palm (top right) stops an attack from above or can be used to attack the arm from below. The back

of the palm is used in the falling palm (bottom left) to pull the attack downward. The overturning palm technique (bottom right) is used to deflect an attack to the outside line.

Face the enemy in the basic stance position.

Many Shan Pi Ta techniques involve trapping or catching the enemy attack. In order to do this properly, it is essential that the principle of redirecting the energy of that attack is understood. (It is said that a "force of a thousand pounds can be deflected by a weight of four ounces.") The Ninja palm can be executed so fast that it permits time for the agent to counterattack before the enemy can move out of range.

Vertical knife hand or rising palm block—From this position, drive straight at the enemy's throat with a spear hand strike by turning the palm down and snapping the fingertips forward.

Palm-up block or lifting palm—This is similar to a Chudan action, except it is much smaller and emphasizes the twist of the wrist. Shift forward and drive a quick finger jab into the enemy's eyes. If you are working from a low stance, use this fist to pinch his triceps from below to paralyze the arm.

Falling palm—Dropping the upturned palm onto the enemy's forearm deflects the attack down and to the side. It may also be quickly turned into a vicious tiger claw strike by merely sliding the palm up the enemy's arm to strike the side of his face.

Overturning palm—Striking quickly downward with the edge of your hand onto the top of the enemy's arm may break the radius. By then turning the hand over to seize the enemy's arm and pressing the points with your thumb and fingers, you may easily pull him to one side.

Kake Uke:
Knife Hand Block

Ninja often have a reputation of being able to throw the enemy aside with a wave of the hand. As with many legends, there is some basis in fact.

The striking surface is the outside edge of the hand; the target is usually the enemy's forearm on the outside line and the biceps on the inside. It is best employed against surprise attacks. The block is very quick and next to jodan is the easiest to learn.

This movement allows one to deflect an attack to the centerline without sidestepping. It is an important tool in creating an opening in the enemy's defense, or it can be used alone to cripple the enemy.

Normally, when one's arm is broken, one falls to the side. Likewise, when the biceps and upper arm are shattered, the enemy is generally considered to be out of the fight.

From the basic back stance, whip the edge of the hand up and out as if wiping a cloth on a mirror. The palm describes a small circle directly in front of the enemy's chest.

The enemy will see the palm come up and think you are making a defensive move. The knife hand strikes the enemy's arm before he can realize it is the intended target.

This strike is not taught in other martial arts and is considered a dirty trick by many.

Face the enemy with the lead hand "cocked" in the sword hand position (top left). With a simple jab, strike the ulnar side of the forearm to break the bone. To do so requires eight pounds of pressure. The blow must be sharp and snappy to be effective (top right). If the enemy steps in with a hooking attack, strike the inside of his forearm with a chop, or slip inside and hit the center of the biceps. A light blow will paralyze the arm; a strong one may break the humerus and rupture the muscle (bottom left). The mirror block

or dig is also effective against kicking attacks. Although most muscles may be "stunned" by a sharp blow to the belly of the muscle, by far the preferred target for a chop to the leg would be the bone. As with the downward sword hand, this attack may be directed at the foot, particularly against the instep of those who are fond of high roundhouse kicks (bottom right).

Cross Chest Block
Low Serpent Parry

This deflection totally protects one side of the body. It may be used against an enemy who seems to favor a one-sided attack to set up the counter; or to withstand the impact of a strong technique on that side. In the field of stealth, this pose is used to press against an object to conceal one's position.

The upper palm protects the head as it shifts to the outside line, away from the attack. Generally, the body is protected by the shoulder and outside of the near arm. The near palm forms a low serpent parry as an adjunct to the movement. The body is also turned away from the attack.

The obvious counterstrike is a roundhouse with the rear leg.

Beginning in the basic back stance, shift the weight toward the attack as it starts, while simultaneously lifting the left hand and pushing across the chest with the out-turned palm and sweeping down and out with the right.

This movement is often coupled with a 180-degree back pivot which, when properly timed, strikes the enemy's shoulder and knocks him aside.

The enemy steps in with a hooking punch to your head. Step to the outside, shifting your weight over your lead leg as you bring your lead hand up in preparation for executing the block.

Slap the enemy's fist to the side by pushing directly across your chest with the left palm. By grabbing his wrist and striking his elbow with your own, it is possible to break his arm with one hand.

Alternately, strike across the line of engagement, hitting the enemy's elbow with the left palm heel strike. This is analogous to jamming the knee with a low push block.

Classical Application of the Reverse Circling Block

The spinning wheel kick is one of the most devastating attacks used by many fighters. In most cases, the defender has little choice but to avoid the blow the best way he can. Circling offers an alternative to this by its use of turning inside the arc of the kick to dissipate its force.

The enemy begins to execute the back-pivot, "sighting" over his shoulder before attacking (top).

As his intent becomes clear, swing your lead arm up and over. Keep the rear hand defensively near the solar plexus (center).

As the kick is thrown, begin to turn into the attack, and drop the arm downward toward the leg.

As the enemy's leg comes under the circular block, trap it between your hip and lead forearm.

Step into a tight stance with the right foot, both feet toe out. Continue to turn into the kick as you further secure a hold on his leg with your right arm.

Continue to turn to your left rear as you pull him further around by his leg.

Drop to the right knee to take your enemy down.

Mawashi Uke:
Reverse Circling

This block consists of a wide circular motion designed to deflect the enemy's attack by redirecting the motion in an ever-increasing arc. It is sim-ilar to the whipping branch parry used in the hidden hand system. It protects a large area with the wide sweeping action. The momentum of the arm whipping from the shoulder lends power to the clamping strike.

Assume a side stance with a low lead guard. Keep the rear hand near the head defensively (top left). As the enemy attack is launched, swing the lead arm in a wide circular arc while falling back slightly (top right). Continue the circular action (bottom left) as you begin to shift your weight toward the front. Complete the arc by whipping the lead hand down and to the outside line (bottom right).

In combat, deceiving the enemy about the gap between your two positions is important. This is accomplished for the most part by the "black-on-black" silhouette which is presented by the costume. You can move as many as ten inches toward or away from the enemy by slowly advancing or withdrawing the hips (hara) over the center of balance. By quickly bending the knees, it will appear as though you are advancing.

The enemy has chambered his kick and strikes out with a high roundhouse kick, intending to hit your temple with the ball of the foot. Drop your open palm toward his rear leg and under his attack. Simultaneously, tuck your chin to your shoulder and raise it defensively.

Entwine the enemy's leg before the kick can land, and clamp onto the back of his knee.

Toe-in with the left foot, and turn your shoulder toward the inside line to throw the enemy down.

Shuto Uke:
Double Sword Hand

Lay the left palm on the right cheek, then pull the hand six inches away from the face. Extend the right fingertips to touch the right ear, then draw them six inches away from the head. Stand in kokutsu dachi or back stance with 40 percent of the weight on the lead leg and 60 percent on the rear leg. Form the fists into sword hands by tensing the outside edge of each palm and bending the thumb down to lock the tension in the hand. The purpose of this block/strike is to knock aside defense or counterattack by the enemy, drive forward with the shoulders to penetrate his sphere, and cut him down with one strike.

Strike out swiftly and strongly with both hands simultaneously as you shift your weight toward the enemy. As the arms whip forward, the lead shoulder will take any attack the enemy may have launched at the same time as yours. Your elbow will then come into play, sweeping the line of engagement clear as you snap the first sword hand out to strike the enemy's throat. At the same time, the right arm defensively protects the head and torso as the shoulders are turned toward the enemy. It is the twisting action of the shoulders and hips which adds power to the double shuto.

Having slashed across the enemy's throat with the left hand, the left arm continues to swing to the outside, clearing the line and defending the body. The right shuto now comes into play as the hips complete their turn into the line. The cutting palm strike attacks the temple with the uplifted edge of the right hand. To practice, let the hands complete their arc and load the double shuto on the left side. Strike back across the line of engagement and repeat on the right. In this way one can "chop the enemies down like wheat."

Face the enemy in a back stance as he assumes a right lead with a low guard. This attack can also be used to "beat the arm down" if the enemy carries a high guard, or to knock aside his attack and strike him before he can withdraw.

Strike out strongly with the leading hand to hit the enemy's trachea or the side of his neck with a reverse chop as your right hand begins its arc toward his head.

The left hand sweeps past his throat, having done its damage to the windpipe or phrenic nerve. The right cutting palm strike drives into his temple.

This technique is most effective when "holding a doorway." The frame will prevent most attacks and the powerful chopping action can be performed in a restricted space to drop the enemy into the opening, thereby making passage difficult.

Mi Shou:
Hidden Hand Technique

Assume a moderately wide horse stance with the left shoulder facing the enemy. Select the target you wish to strike, and form the right fist into the appropriate "hand/weapon." Lower your center and place the fist at this point.

Cover the right fist with the open left hand, concealing it from the enemy much as a baseball pitcher hides the ball from the batter (below).

Tuck your chin into your shoulder defensively; fix the enemy's eye with your stare (top right).

Sweep outward and upward with the left hand, batting aside the enemy guard or defense with the whipping branch parry. Temporarily distract him with the lead hand (center right). Keep the left side to the enemy, as it presents the smallest target.

Kiai as you step forward. Turn the shoulders and hips simultaneously to add impact to the punch (bottom right). Drive your fist into the target with all your strength. The kiai is a "spirit shout" which enables you to draw upon the source of your inner strength. This results in *kime* or focus to the strike and makes it doubly effective. Furthermore, the sudden scream of total commitment often startles the enemy, freezing him for a critical second when the battle is won or lost.

Stand in the side stance with the left side toward the enemy. The left hand covers the right fist so that the enemy cannot see which fist has been isometrically shaped by the right hand.

Strike out swiftly with the left hand in the whipping branch parry to deflect his attack, or beat down his guard and direct his attention to the left hand.

Turn into the punch with your shoulders and hips as you strike out with the right fist. Here we have used the sun fist strike to the chin, which drives the enemy's head straight back and stuns the brainstem. Other strikes might be the small tiger mouth strike to the throat or the spear hand strike to the solar plexus.

There are nine such specific "fists" which form the hidden hand system, all of which may be delivered as shown.

Hidden Hand:
Palm Heel Strike

Drive upward with the heel of the right hand, driving the enemy's head back (top). This not only stuns the brain stem by whiplash action, but also jams the teeth together and shatters them. This attack may be followed quite easily with a downward finger rip across the eyes to blind the enemy.

Hidden Hand:
Small Tiger Mouth Strike

The head and throat are the favorite targets of the hidden hand, since the enemy most often reacts to the parry by dropping his left shoulder and tucking in his elbow protectively. This, of course, exposes his upper line. Drive forward from the shoulder with the fist, and strike the enemy with the web of the hand between the extended thumb and curled fingers (center). As the fingers sink in, seize the windpipe in a powerful grip and peel the trachea out of the neck to kill.

Hidden Hand:
Follow-up Technique

In the unlikely event that the first strike does not finish the enemy, drop the left hand back across your centerline to deflect any counterattack (bottom). Chop to the enemy's temple with the right hand to render him unconscious.

The classical hidden hand has only nine targets, all on the enemy centerline, and nine fists, two of which are kicks.

Tsuan-Uke:
The Uppercut

When properly performed, this has much the same effect as the palm heel strike. In the hidden hand system, the fist is placed against the enemy's chest and slides straight up to strike from below. This makes it virtually impossible to block.

Offensive Strikes 6

The target area is the xyphoid process, which is located at the lower tip of the sternum. This tiny triangular bone is held in place by a thin hinge of cartilage, riding up and down with the rib cage. Directly behind this bone lies the large diaphragm muscle, which controls respiration. At this point, where the phrenic nerve enters the diaphragm, the layers of tissue covering the ribs and chest are the weakest.

Attacking the solar plexus is performed by forming the fore-fist and placing it palm up at the level of the armpit. The punch is launched by driving the fist forward and twisting the hand over in mid-flight. The striking surface is again the first two knuckles. The angle of the blow is slightly downward, which adds body weight to the action and lends snap to the punch.

A light tap near the lower frontal ribs will cause a slight contraction of the diaphragm and the intercostal muscles between the ribs, which take over the respiratory function in situations of stress. A hard blow to the diaphragm or ribs will relax these muscles for a moment. When relaxed, the muscles force air out of the lungs, continuing to squeeze until the muscles let the ribs expand again for inhalation. Unconsciousness due to mechanical respiratory paralysis induced by a blow to the xyphoid process is the result of this strike.

Inno-Uke:
Striking the Scrotum

The second most vulnerable area of the body is the groin, which includes the penis, testicles, scrotum, bladder, and central portion of the pubic bone. The forward snap kick is the single most effective weapon for attacking the groin. It allows you to keep distance between you and the assailant, and is therefore a long-range weapon.

Rupture of the bladder wall from the percussive shock of a solid kick or a fracture of the pubic bone, blood and urine in the abdominal cavity, and tenderness and pain are the least one can expect from a kick to this area. The center of the pelvis is the weakest and most probable point of fracture. Inability to walk because of the pinching and abraiding pain of the pubic bones rubbing together will leave the attacker doubled in a prone position, with arms across the abdomen.

For the kick to penetrate to the underside of the frontal pelvis, it must first drive through the penis and the scrotum. As these are soft tissues, this is not difficult. Disruption of the urethra and bleeding and urine in the scrotum will be the minimum injuries. Such contamination of the body cavity holds the possibility of infection and peritonitis.

The testicles are very mobile within the scrotum. Pain, shock, loss of breath, nausea, vomiting, and unconsciousness, but rarely death, follow such an attack.

Kiri-Uke:
Attacking the Throat

The target area lies from the underside of the chin to the jugular notch between the clavicles. Striking the neck from the front, back, or side can set an attacker off balance and breathless. The weapon used is the hand sword, which is created by extending the fingers, knuckles together, and tensing them upward to harden the edge of the hand. The thumb is then cocked to create the proper tension for the attack. The internal jugular vein distends during exhalation and collapses during inhalation. If the strike occurs as the opponent exhales, the artery will be full of blood and semi-rigid. Rupturing the vessel by driving it into the surface of the cervical vertebrae will result in death due to massive blood loss.

An attack to this area can also damage the vagus nerve, which lies within the carotid sheath and controls heart contraction and lung constriction. While it is unlikely that a single blow will damage both branches of this important nerve, injury to one side will cause lung and heart spasms, ultimately leading to shortness of breath, heart palpitations, and death.

The phrenic nerve, which runs from the fourth cervical vertebrae down the neck, controls breathing reflexes. The immediate effect of an attack is the feeling that the wind has been knocked out of the chest. This condition will persist until normal functioning is restored by massage or resuscitation. Unless this is done, death from oxygen starvation will result.

Mu-Uke:
Striking the Eye

A torn eyelid, in most cases the upper one, is the minimum damage one should expect from this attack. A sharp fingernail piercing the eyelid that has closed at the last possible instant will cause such an injury. Aside from temporary blindness and eye trauma, infection is also likely from small debris (dirt, germs, or hair) which enters the eye with the finger and nail. This can be a more serious complication than the strike itself.

To apply the twin dragon strike, grasp the opponent behind the head with the left hand. Execute an upward fingertip strike to the eyes with the index and middle fingers. Drive the fingers into the eyes and follow through until the attacker is overcome. The probable result of this attack is rupture of the eye bulb with protrusion of the watery and gelatinous contents. This results in permanent blindness.

To execute the thumb gouge, grasp the opponent's head firmly in both hands, palms covering the ears, and simultaneously gouge the thumbs into the eye sockets. This will either rupture the eye or force the eye bulb from the socket.

Kappo
Introduction

There are two kinds of secret teachings in the ancient art of NienJihTsu. One is Dim Mak, the death touch, and the other is Kappo, the art of resuscitation. The remnants of this elaborate art are seen in judo today, but few fully comprehend its origins.

Each technique is designed to revive an individual rendered unconscious by a blow to a specific target. Many Ninja find employment in medical fields, since fully half their art was once healing in nature. One strives to learn Kappo not so that an enemy can be killed and brought back to life, although this is possible and was once a preferred method for dealing with intruders. Rather, the student seeks to relieve the suffering of his fellow man, be it caused by the inevitable turn of the wheel of fate or by the necessity to inflict injury to avoid being harmed oneself. Knowledge of medicinal techniques may be of great value in the field should one be injured or if the state of the enemy's health is in question.

The admonition to know thyself applies equally to the physical realm as the mental, for certainly the two are inseparable. Learn these simple lessons well. They are the foundation of the greater skills which lie ahead.

Level of Unconsciousness

In a legal choke, unconsciousness results as the air supply is cut off. This can be checked by noting the reaction of the pupils to light, which should be checked periodically during any form of resuscitation. It provides the best indication of delivery of oxygenated blood to the patient's brain. Pupils that constrict when exposed to light indicate adequate oxygenation and blood flow. Pupils that remain widely dilated and do not react to light indicate serious brain damage is imminent or has already occurred. Dilated but reactive pupils are less ominous. Normal pupillary reaction may alter naturally in the aged or in any individual by the administration of drugs.

The basic steps of artificial respiration are a) to open the airway, and b) to restore breathing. These steps constitute emergency first aid for airway obstruction and respiratory inadequacy or failure.

Respiratory inadequacy may result from an

obstruction of the airway or from respiratory failure. An obstructed airway is sometimes difficult to recognize until the airway itself is opened. At other times, a partially obstructed airway may be recognized by labored breathing or excessive respiratory efforts.

Respiratory failure is characterized by absence of respiratory effort, failure of the chest or upper abdomen to move, and inability to detect air movement through the nose or mouth.

The most important factor in resuscitation is immediate opening of the airway. In the unconscious patient, lying in a supine position, the relaxed muscles may allow the lower jaw to drop backward. Since the tongue is attached to the mandible and the floor of the mouth, it can obstruct the back of the throat. This obstruction can be easily and quickly cleared by tilting the head backward as far as possible. Sometimes this simple maneuver is all that is required for breathing to resume spontaneously.

To perform the head tilt, position the patient on his back. Place one hand beneath the patient's neck and the other hand on his forehead. Lift the neck with one hand and tilt the head backward, applying pressure on the forehead with the other hand. This maneuver extends the neck and lifts the tongue away from the back of the throat. The head must be maintained in this position at all times.

When the patient is in this position, with his head tilted back, you should *look, listen,* and *feel* to determine if there is respiration. Place your cheek close to the patient's mouth and nose. *Look* at the chest and upper abdomen to see if they rise and fall; *listen* and *feel* for expelling air. If there is no evidence of spontaneous respiration, resuscitation should begin.

Cardiac arrest is recognized by no pulse in the large arteries of an unconscious patient, a death-like appearance and absence of breathing. The fingernails may also become bluish; this condition is known as cyanosis. The status of the carotid artery pulse should be checked as quickly as possible when cardiac arrest is suspected. Open the airway and quickly ventilate the lungs four times. Maintain the head tilt with one hand on the forehead, and use the tips of the index and middle fingers of the other hand to locate the patient's larynx (Adam's apple). Slide the fingers laterally into the groove between the trachea and the muscles at the side of the neck where the carotid artery can be felt. The pulse must be felt gently, not compressed.

It is not advisable to check pupillary reaction as an indication of cardiac arrest prior to initiating resuscitation. This often leads to uncertainty and delay in starting effective treatment. Absence of the carotid pulse should be the only criterion for diagnosing cardiac arrest.

Cardiopulminary resuscitation, also known as CPR, is a combination of artificial respiration and artificial circulation, which should be started immediately when cardiac arrest occurs. It has been widely and successfully used by doctors, nurses and allied health personnel. Persons engaging in body contact sports such as the martial arts should not only be trained in the Oriental methods of resuscitation, but should further attend the first aid and CPR courses offered on a regular basis by the American Red Cross.

Art of Resuscitation

Resuscitation means to bring back to life, back to the senses, back to consciousness. There are scores of resuscitation methods for all types of emergencies. Only a few are explained here, but they are sufficient for most needs.

The requirements for success in this work are:

1) Proper treatment—which comes from study;

2) Coolness—which comes from understanding proper treatment and knowing that the method is correct;

3) Confidence—which comes from practice.

Remember—when you treat a patient with one method and it does not seem to succeed, try another method and continue until you do succeed.

Revival from Unconsciousness

Even when unconsciousness is the result of a legal choke (against the carotid artery), there is danger of serious injury if the patient is not revived in a short time. Brain damage could occur within eight minutes.

To revive a groggy person, not fully unconscious but also not functioning normally, place him in a seated position and strike sharply downward between the shoulder blades. Use the heel of the palm and direct the blow so that the pressure goes in the direction of his abdomen. Repeat once or twice. Loosen his belt and let him lie down and revive. In addition, if unconsciousness is the result of a choke, massage the sides of the neck in an upward direction with the fingertips.

Usually, an unconscious person is limp and relaxed. Occasionally, however, he may become rigid. In this case, be very careful how you move him; do not try to force the arms or legs out of a rigid position, but rather move them slowly and gently, exerting steady pressure.

Hsi-Katsu:
The Heart Method

The second method of reviving a person who is unconscious from strangulation, from a blow, or from a heavy fall begins by lifting the patient to a sitting position as before. Brace your knee against his spine. Bring his left hand across his chest and under his right armpit. Hold his left shoulder lightly with your left hand and pull on his left arm with your right hand to force the air out of his chest. Apply pressure gradually, then release it suddenly to allow the chest to expand and draw in more air. Continue pumping gently ten to fifteen times a minute. Once the faintest sign of respiration is observed, the pumping must be timed to reinforce it. Stop as soon as the patient starts breathing independently. Frequently only one or two contractions and releases will do the trick. If the person has been out for some time, as many as thirty may be required. After the patient begins breathing, pound him ten times between the shoulder blades with the heel of a half-closed loose fist.

Fei-Katsu:
The Lung Method

The third method involves crossing the patient's arms in front of his chest, right arm on top. Stand behind the patient, holding the right arm at the wrist and elbow. Brace your knee against his spine. Now squeeze his chest against your knee, slowly forcing the air out. Suddenly release the chest, allowing it to expand and draw in more air. Continue pumping at the normal breathing rate. Stop as soon as the patient starts breathing, then pound between the shoulder blades.

Sasoi-Katsu:
The Inductive Method

In this method, stand behind the patient who is seated in a cross-legged position, and support him from behind by placing the kneecap of the right leg against the patient's spine with the knee bent and the heel raised. Place the hands, with the fingers spread outward, over the lower part of the chest so that the fingers hook in under the lowest ribs on each side. Pull the chest upward and backward steadily as if to open the chest cavity toward both sides with the weight of the body on the arms. Bend the upper part of the body backwards and straighten the knee with the heel now on the floor. Thus raise the ribs, enlarge the chest cavity and force air to enter to imitate inhalation. When the ribs have been pulled upward to the utmost extent, release them gently, allowing them to return to their former position, expelling the air to imitate exhalation. Repeat this procedure until respiration is restored.

So-Katsu:
The Composite Method

In the fifth method, the patient is laid on his back. Kneel astride his hips and place the hands with fingers spread and pointing upward over the lower part of the chest wall. Press upward against the chest to imitate exhalation. Then rock backward to allow the elastic recoil of the chest wall to imitate inhalation. Use only enough strength to force out the air. Continue this action at the normal breathing rate until respiration is restored, then sit the patient in an upright position and pound between the shoulder blades as before.

Jinzo-Katsu:
The Kidney Method

The Jinzo-Katsu method involves placing the patient face down. The operator kneels astride the patient's hips and places his hands about halfway down against the patient's back. Press straight downward, forcing out the air, and then suddenly release the pressure in order to allow the chest to expand. More air is thus drawn in. Continue this procedure at the rate of normal breathing until respiration is restored. Sit the patient upright, and pound as before. Note that the pressure in this method is directed straight downward; in the So-Katsu technique, it is directed forward (toward the shoulders).

Kiri-Katsu:
The Head Method

The Kiri-Katsu technique is used primarily to revive a person who has been rendered unconscious by a blow to the head. Sit the patient upright. The four fingers of your right hand should be placed against the patient's right temple, and the left fingers against the left temple. Place your right thumb against the hollow space at the base of the back side of his neck (just behind the ear and just below the base of the skull). Place your left thumb in a similar position at the back left side of his neck.

In a kneading action, massage his temples and the back of his neck by revolving your fingers and thumbs three times in a circular motion with medium pressure. With a little more pressure, lift his head up by your fingertips, as if you were going to lift his head off his body. Suddenly take away all pressure by removing your hands from his head. Repeat this technique a few times. When the patient revives, strike him between the shoulders as before to stimulate nervous action. If he does not respond, use one of the other methods described herein. In the case of head blows, although respiration may be impeded, artificial respiration should be withheld because of the danger of concussion and the risk of serious inflammation of the brain. The patient should be put to bed at once with the head low and kept warm. Stimulants, except in special cases, should be withheld. Excitement should be avoided, and for some time after apparent recovery, care is needed. It is advisable to send for a physician while first aid is administered, and to take care in noting signs of shock.

Eri-Katsu:
The Lapels Method

In this method, the patient is embraced in the left arm and inclined a little from the hips. From a kneeling position on the patient's right side, place the right palm with four fingers together on the lower abdomen just above the navel and press upward against the solar plexus, raising the diaphragm and chest wall, decreasing the chest cavity and expelling the air to imitate exhalation. Simultaneously bend the upper part of the patient's body forward to supplement this action. Release the chest wall gently by a slow, receding movement, allowing it to return to its first position, enlarging the chest cavity and causing air to enter, imitating inhalation. Repeat until respiration is restored.

To administer restoratives or medicine, embrace the patient as before, place the palm of the left hand on his forehead and pull the lower

jaw downward with the right hand until the mouth is opened. Administer the restorative, close the mouth, and hold it shut with the left hand; stroke the throat in a downward direction to cause swallowing, and proceed with the technique.

Ke-Katsu:
The Groin Method

These techniques are recommended in cases involving injury to the testicles. In the first case, the patient has been struck an accidental blow to the groin. He is not unconscious, but is in intense pain. Have the patient place himself in a natural stance with the feet about a shoulder-width apart. With the legs slightly bent, but rigid and spread, have the patient jump up and land on the heels so that the body is jarred. Repeat once or twice. Massage the lower abdomen in a downward direction. The purpose of this technique is to jolt the testes down into their normal position.

Kogan-Katsu:
The Testicle Method

A heavy blow to the testicles will sometimes force them up into the body as well as cause unconsciousness. This technique is meant to release the testes.

Place the patient on his back, handling him very gently. Kneel at his leg, grip his big toe, and raise his leg up and slightly outward on the affected side. With the heel of your fist, strike sharply at the heel of his foot. Repeat once or twice. Repeat on the other leg, if necessary. Once release has been effected, sit the patient upright with his arm around your neck. Your left arm supports him. Place your right hand against his lower abdomen on either side, but preferably in the center to make sure that you relieve whichever side is affected. Now, quickly slide your hand downward several times to restore the testes to their proper position. Usually this will revive the patient, but if he remains unconscious, switch to any of the other methods, except those which utilize an upward striking action.

Inno-Katsu:
The Scrotum Method

The following technique is intended for use when unconsciousness is caused by a heavy blow to the testicles. Place the patient in a seated position, legs slightly spread. From a crouching position behind him, thrust your hands and arms under his armpits and lock your forearms together. Lift him in the air a little and let him drop so that he lands squarely on the buttocks. Repeat once or twice, or until the testes have resumed their proper position. It is also effective if, standing behind the patient, you lightly kick the lower lumbar vertebrae with the ball of the foot.

Weapons 7

The following are but a few of the many deadly devices of the Ninja. While the practitioners of the art of ninjitsu are known as weapons masters, most ryu specialize in one or two and teach the others as corollary training aids. Remember, it is not the weapon which is dangerous, but the man who wields it.

WEAPONS DETAIL

1. Ninja Walking Staff (wooden)
2. Replica Ninja Sword
3. Replica Scabbard with Cord
4. Lotus Style Shuriken
5. Traditional Short Sword
6. Traditional Garrote
7. Traditional Ninja Sword
8. Five Elements Shuriken
9. Traditional Daito
10. Three-Point Shuriken
11. Traditional Sais
12. Black Dragon Ax
13. Traditional Kama
14. Stiletto Style Knife
15. Six-Point Shuriken
16. Ninja Equipment Case
17. Ninja Crowbar
18. Kusari-Fundo
19. Eight-Point Shuriken
20. Hide-a-Chuck (Hanbo)
21. Extend-a-Chuck
22. Extend-a-Chuck Case
23. Ninja Pouch
24. Grappling Hook with Line
25. Kyoketsu-Shogi with Line
26. Three Throwing Knives
27. Traditional Nunchaku
28. Concealed Knife
29. Yawara
30. Ceremonial Sword

In this section we shall touch on a few of the items illustrated above. Many good texts exist on most of them, so we shall dwell primarily on the more obscure elements. We briefly mention the sword due to its historical importance in Japanese culture.

Ninja-To

The ninja-to, or sword of darkness, is the third type of sword found in kenjitsu. It is the product of a fertile imagination and is extremely functional. Unlike the daito or shuto which may have been decorated in numerous ways to the satisfaction of its owner, the ninja-to is totally devoid of any decorative design. It serves not only as a weapon, but also as a tool of its master. The scabbard is longer than the blade and can be used as a club or mace, a device for concealing objects, and, in conjunction with the inserted blade, as a ladder rung. The scabbard is open at both ends, allowing it to be employed as a blowgun or as a snorkel-like breathing tube. Unlike the daito and shuto, which have curved blades, the ninja-to is straight. The handguard is larger than the conventional tsubo and generally rectangular in shape. This serves as a foothold if the sword is leaned against a wall. Once the summit has been reached, the sword is drawn up to its owner by means of the attached cord. This cord can also serve as a tourniquet in the event of an injury.

Naturally this does not exhaust the types of sword found in the Orient. Notably absent is the broadsword, but this is primarily of Chinese origin and is used in a one-hand style. Likewise, there are numerous smaller-bladed weapons, dirks, daggers, and so on, but these, too, have been omitted since they are not used in the two-hand style. The technique which follows applies equally to all of the three sword types. The terminology and target areas are identical.

The traditional method of wearing the sword is shown here.

Loop the end of the sayo over the end of the scabbard.

Pull the center of the sayo to form a loop as shown.

Slip the loop over the shoulder.

Hold the end of the scabbard when carrying the weapon.

Over-Shoulder Draw

Confronted by the enemy, remember that the sword is effectively hidden behind your extended arm. Even if he might be armed, seeing the weapon in your hand may cause him to try to take some action to subdue rather than kill.

Hide the sword behind your extended arm (top).

Using the hold on the scabbard, tilt the sword so that the handle is brought to a position near the left ear (center). Grip the sword hilt by reaching across your chest with the right hand.

Bring the sword to a horizontal position over the left shoulder. Aim the hilt directly at the enemy. In so doing, the silhouette is further distorted, making the weapon more difficult to see.

As the sword clears the scabbard, slightly relax your grip so that the shoulder loop gains a little slack (above). By now the enemy will have begun to react by raising his arms defensively. Even if he gets his guard up (below), the attack will cut deeply into his arms, as well as cut his head or neck. Should your enemy use a sai or other implement to stop the cut, whip the scabbard off the shoulder. Use it as a short staff to hit the enemy in the ribs.

The walking staff is composed of a hollow tube that is filled with a chain twice as long as the staff.

A lead weight, heavy enough to inflict serious injury, is attached to one end.

An open metal hook is attached to the other end.

Shinobi Zue: The Ninja Walking Staff

This is one of the most versatile Ninja weapons. The staff is constructed as follows: a hollow tube is filled with a flexible chain equal to twice its length. To one end is attached a lead weight of sufficient mass to inflict serious injury on one struck by it. To the other end is attached an open metal hook. The contemporary model is equipped with a small hood to cover the hook end, and a rubber cap to cover the weighted end when not in use. The beauty of this device is that each half of the chain counterbalances the other, making it possible to quickly feed either weapon back into the tube to conceal it. Only one end may be used at a time in most techniques.

The shinobi zue is essentially nine weapons in one. It may be employed as a grappling hook using the open hook end to snare a fold of uniform; it may be used as a lasso or a chain whip, using the weighted end. This end also serves as a flail or mace. The staff itself may be used for defense; the chain, when removed from the tube, makes an excellent *manriki-kusari,* and can easily act as a garrote. Last, the hollow staff itself may be employed as a blowgun for launching poison darts, or a snorkel for underwater retreats.

More ancient models were fitted with blades which sprang out to spear the enemy when the tube was twisted. Some modern innovations are the use of the four-prong grapple in place of the single open hook, as well as the quick snap-off release which permits the chain to be withdrawn from the tube.

As a concealed weapon, the staff was often used by Ninja in disguise. The old beggar, the priest, or the lame often employed a staff in walking. In some instances, it was a badge of office. Furthermore, those who follow the disciplines of the staff, such as aikido, are notably non-belligerent. What better disguise for a man with murderous intent?

Use of the Shinobi Zue Lead Weight

Grip the Ninja walking staff in the classic spear "on guard" stance, with the weighted end exposed as the weapon.

Swing your weight back and to the right to gather momentum for the low leg sweep. In actual combat, this may be accomplished by feinting a "butt-stroke" with the free end.

Swing your weight from the back to the front toward the enemy's lead leg at knee level.

Guide the weighted chain toward the enemy's leg by the action of the right hand. The lead leg is always a legitimate target for the Ninja.

The weighted chain hits his leg at knee level. The weight will continue to swing around the leg, but its arc radius will be shortened and it will wrap quickly around the leg.

As the weight whips around your opponent's leg and comes to the end of the chain, it will drop. If the leg is struck with about one foot of chain, there will be enough chain to encircle the target and "lock" over the chain to form a snare.

With the chain wrapped around your enemy's leg, lift the far end of the staff to take up any slack. Draw the chain tight.

Using the leverage provided by the staff, jerk the leg upward and across your enemy's path. This is easy to do if most of his weight is on his rear leg. If he is leaning forward, jab the far end of the staff at his face to make him lean back.

As the enemy takes a backfall, spin the free end of the staff back into the line of attack by taking a step forward with the left foot. Drive the butt end of the staff into his chest.

Other Techniques Using the Lead Weight

With practice, the weight can be hurled at your enemy's head by making the chain loose enough to fall out of the tube, unless the cap is in place, then whipping the staff toward the target. A little practice can make one deadly accurate with this missile.

Otherwise, acting as a flail, the weight may be used simply to beat the enemy senseless.

Swing the end of the staff diagonally across the line of engagement, causing the flail to follow in an erratic arc, striking the enemy on the left side of the neck.

A horizontal arc might also be employed. Even if the enemy blocks with his left arm, the weight will still "wrap" and strike him on the side or back of the head.

The follow-through of the first strike is shown. The head is the preferred target for the flail, since the weapon is hard to see, hard to block, and provides a stunning blow. The psychological impact alone will keep most adversaries at bay.

Occasionally, it becomes necessary to "stand the man back up" for the next strike. To do so, sweep the end of the staff up and under, striking your opponent on the right cheek.

The weighted end of the staff describes a full circle around the Ninja's head. It is brought to bear in a downward strike to the neck exactly like the first strike, but on the other side.

Having been clubbed into submission, the enemy falls. The Ninja "loads" the staff in preparation for the coup de grace if required.

The Hook as Entangling Tool

As an "entangling tool," the Ninja staff uses the open hook end of the chain. Unlike the weight, this implement is too light to be employed as a missile.

Whip the chain toward the enemy in a sweeping overhead strike (left), allowing all of the chain to play out of the staff as you execute the movement.

The hook, in ancient times a four-prong type of grapple, becomes lodged in the enemy's uniform. Pull back on the staff to set the hook. The older grappling hook might just as easily have dug into the flesh.

A close-up of the hook being entangled in the ghi is shown at the bottom left.

Below: The enemy has seized the chain to relieve the pressure of the grapple. Immediately push forward with the end of the staff as if to strike him in the solar plexus, thereby causing him to lock his left arm straight.

Describe a vertical circle with the end of the staff, wrapping the chain around the enemy's left wrist.

Using the leverage of the staff and the painful wrist lock, jerk the enemy's arm down and across the line of engagement. At the same time, take a short step forward with the right foot, thereby closing the distance between the two of you.

After the enemy falls, raise the staff above the prone form of the enemy. This will turn him more onto his back. Drive the near end of the staff (the one from which the chain is released) downward onto his heart or throat as a finishing blow.

The Hook as Lasso

Describe a small arc above the head with the end of the staff by holding the right hand fixed and circling with the left (top left).

This action will cause the chain to execute a wide swinging circle above the heads of both combatants (center left). Allow the full length of the chain to play out of the staff as this movement is executed, thereby increasing the weapon's range.

Drop the end of the staff slightly at the proper moment for the chain to strike the enemy on the neck and wrap around his head (bottom left). Practice this by setting up a post at head level.

As the open hook swings back into the line of engagement, dip the end of the staff and catch the hook on the chain (below). The lasso thus made can just as easily be let go by flipping the hook off.

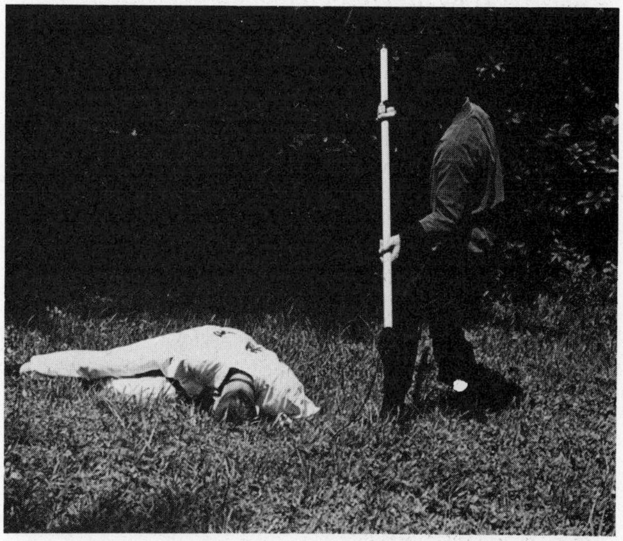

Lift the end of the staff, drawing the noose taut (below). The action of the chain on your opponent's neck will be quite painful. He will seek to ease the choke hold by grabbing at the chain.

Pull strongly downward and across the line of engagement with the end of the staff (top right). Use the leverage of the staff by pulling with the right hand and pushing with the left.

The enemy strikes the ground (center right). Quickly slide-step forward, allowing a small amount of slack to develop in the chain.

Strike the enemy on the back of the head or neck with the far end of the staff (bottom right). Note: This action will jerk the chain taut around the enemy's throat as well.

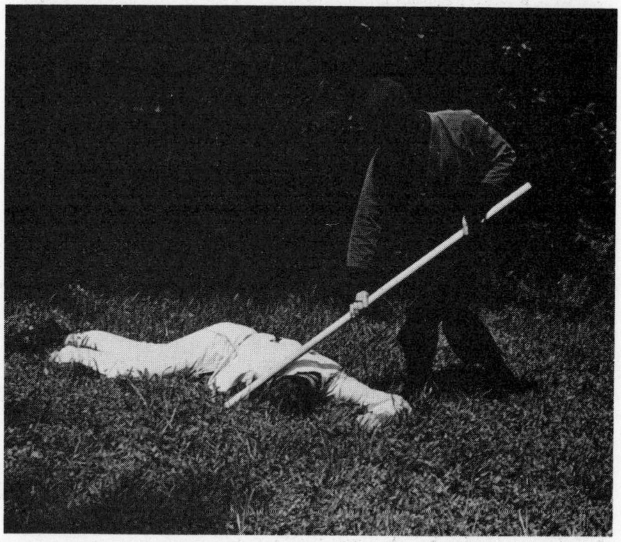

Kyoketsu Shogi:
The Retrievable Stone

It is believed that the Australian bushmen invented the forerunner of the modern yo-yo by tying a circular piece of stone, or a rock with a hole in it, to a length of light cord. When not in use, the line could be wound around the stone out of the way. The cord needed of necessity to be lighter than the ring at the end, so it did not impede throwing the rock at the target. It could be so fine, in fact, that it was almost invisible, especially if made of braided human hair, as were those of the ancient Ninja. Such a rope was far stronger and more flexible than any conventional cord could have been. By practicing the wrist snap explained elsewhere, it was possible to make the stone fly back into the hands of its owner. If the line was not seen, one would seem to possess the magical retrievable stone.

The retrievable stone or ring may be thrown at the enemy as a stunning missile. Numerous techniques were also developed for entangling the enemy in the line after he was stunned by the rock, but capture was seldom on the mind of the Ninja. Having trussed the enemy, he would attack with the deadly double-pointed knife. This is a particularly vicious weapon with two blades set at right angles to each other, the more horizontal of the two curved into a slight hook, making it all the more wicked during infighting.

The double-pointed knife was sometimes called the spider knife. Almost all of the cuts executed with this device involve two motions. When the vertical blade is held in the conventional grip (point above the thumb), the hook is used to cut downward on the enemy's neck, then the point is thrust upward into the stomach or belly. When the shogi was held in the ice-pick grip (point under little finger side of fist), one would first stab downward onto the chest aiming for the heart, then cut outward and horizontally across the stomach with the hook.

Unlike most other Ninja weapons, the kyoketsu shogi has few uses as a tool. The cord could be looped through the ring and used as a lasso, but this is better suited to attaching the cord to something and climbing down rather than throwing, since the ring usually deforms the loop in flight. The sayo or line may also be used to trap, ensnare, tie, or choke the enemy.

In the stance shown below, the knife would be the primary weapon. The coils of rope and the ring could be thrown or used as a flail, but normally, the stone was thrown with one hand while the line was allowed to play out from the other.

The ready position is shown above.

Casting the Ring

In "casting" the ring, note that the wrist is curled.

In releasing the ring, the fingers are extended and the wrist is "snapped."

In the throw, the ring flies toward the target, carrying the line along with it.

The ring has carried the line as far as possible: the line "feeds" out from the loose coils in the left hand. Grip the line lightly in the right hand and take up the slack (top left).

The ring flies back toward the Ninja's hand (center left). Snap the line upward (bottom left) and back by flicking the wrist. The ring is caught with the free hand and is ready to be launched again (bottom).

The Ring as Weapon

Hold the hook-knife and several coils of line in the left hand. The ring should be held between the fingers of the right hand.

Throw the ring toward your enemy's face, making him move out of position to avoid being hit. Allow the line to play out from the coils in the left hand.

The object is not so much to strike the enemy, but rather to make him seize the line—the first step leading to his downfall.

Flip a coil of the line over the enemy's head by shifting the weight forward and describing a counterclockwise circle with the right hand. This action is transmitted to the slack formed by closing the gap and is carried over the head by the momentum of the rope.

The enemy's right hand is now pinned to his head. Snake a length of line around his arm in a similar manner. Both arms are now entangled. Let the line play out of the left hand as needed.

Draw the line taut by pulling down and across the line of engagement.

Advance on the enemy by stepping forward and to the left with the left foot. Wrap the line around the enemy's head, thereby drawing his left arm up near his face. Note: All of these techniques (the flip, snake, and wrap) are accomplished by describing the same counterclockwise circle with the right hand.

The takedown is performed by swinging the left arm far to the rear of the right, pivoting on the ball of the right foot, and jerking roughly downward on the remaining length of line. Note that the "pull" is directed ninety degrees to the enemy's line of balance.

The impact of the enemy striking the ground face first, without being able to break his fall, should be sufficient to stun him. The coup de grace may be delivered with the hook knife, or you may strangle him with the line.

The Cord as Snare

Drop a loop of the cord through the open ring to form a noose, concealing it in the enemy's path. The enemy has stepped into the loop (top left) with his right foot.

Jerk the noose tight, and pull the enemy's leg across his own path to trip him (center left).

Use both hands to jerk the enemy off his feet if need be, causing him to fall on his right side (bottom left).

Drop on the enemy from above. Finish him with the hook knife as shown, or continue to entangle him with the line so he may be captured (below).

The Hook Knife

The advantage of any weapon with a chain or line is that it allows the user to remain at long range from the enemy. Such weapons were therefore often employed when one was forced to engage a swordsman.

However, the hook knife, based on the farmer's hand sickle, was used almost entirely for infighting and slashing the enemy to ribbons.

With the enemy's arm blocked or entangled, use the conventional grip and stab him straight in the belly. This does not always create a wound that will kill, but the psychological effect is quite devastating.

Withdraw the knife by crossing the line of the engagement with the right hand in preparation for the next cut.

Strike down on the right side of the enemy's neck with the "sickle" or hook portion of the weapon (top left), slashing the carotid artery.

Follow through with the neck cut (center left).

Turn the palm outward and cut back into the left side of the enemy's neck with the hook edge (bottom left). This severs the carotid artery on that side.

Reverse your grip on the hook knife, changing to the "ice-pick grip" (the point of the knife extending out from under the little finger). The hook is on the finger side of the fist (below).

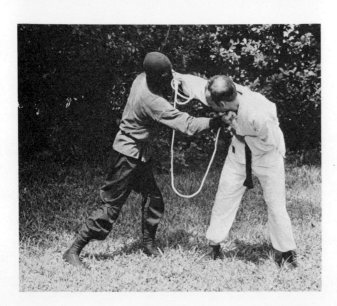

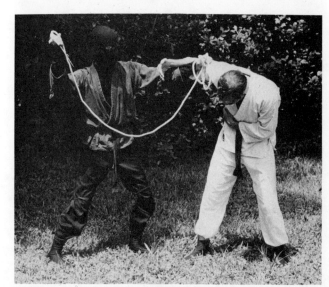

Turn the palm up and cut horizontally across the belly with the hook (below). This cut is usually directed to the abdomen, and is similar to the hara-kiri cut.

Turn the palm down and cut back upward into the throat (top right). Unlike previous cuts, this cut is directed to the trachea, or windpipe.

Follow through with the throat cut and "load" the knife near the right ear (center right).

Stab directly downward (bottom right), driving the blade deep into the enemy's heart.

There are six cuts shown in this practice form (two with the blade and four with the hook edge). All six may be performed against the enemy in less than five seconds.

Tonki:
Edged Throwing Weapons

Shurikens and the throwing knife, easily concealed, can be used to injure or possibly kill an opponent.

The shuriken can be gripped by the tip.

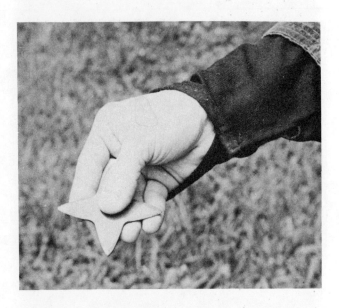

It can also be gripped by the flat of the blade.

Hip Pocket Throw

Draw the shuriken from the hip pocket, holding it in the flat grip slightly behind the right hip. This keeps it out of the enemy's view.

Whip the arm out from the side in a quarter-arc, releasing the weapon horizontally with a snap of the wrist. This imparts a spinning action to the shuriken.

The spinning disc digs into the enemy's neck.

The neck is the target of choice for this throw since the enemy's front is exposed and he is just out of fist range.

Heart Throw

This is an excellent close-range throw. Holding the knife by the flat of the blade (top left), throw it with a classic axe type motion from a spot near the right ear. This is a powerful action, as it must be to penetrate the enemy's chest.

Release the knife with the thumb pointing directly at the enemy's heart, while the blade is in horizontal position (center left). The knife will rotate half a turn, striking the target point first.

The knife strikes. The blade, being horizontal, slips easily between the ribs (bottom left) to a depth sufficient to pierce the heart (below).

Temple Throw

Holding the shuriken by one of the tips, throw it strongly with a downward whipping type of action, snapping the wrist on the release to make the weapon spin (below). Release the shuriken when the index finger points directly at the temple side of the enemy's head. Next, snap the wrist (top right).

The weapon strikes the enemy (center right). The sharp hooked points can easily drive through the thin layer of bone at this site (bottom right). As in the previous technique, this is a powerful throw and can be used over much greater distance than has been shown.

The Classic Knife Throw

Unlike the flat throw in which the knife rotates only a half turn, the knife in this method may spin many times. Only practice will make one capable of successfully using this technique.

Holding the knife by the tip, throw it from the shoulder (top left) with a strong whipping motion.

Snap the wrist (as in the shuriken release) when the index finger points at the base of the enemy's skull (center left).

The range for this throw must be determined by the practitioner. It is a very strong throw which allows excellent penetration (bottom left).

The blade drives into the base of the enemy's skull (below).

Chan Sheng:
The Rope of War

Basically, the genin agent's work in the field is intelligence gathering. To achieve this, he must sometimes come very close to the enemy. At times he must penetrate the enemy encampment for the purposes of sabotage, and at other times the mission may involve terminating an individual. Since the hallmark of the Ninja is silence, they stress methods which eliminate the enemy quickly and quietly. To this end, genin are trained in the use of the chan sheng, or rope of war. This device is also used by other services and may be seen on parade uniforms as the French Croix de Guerre.

It is said that the Spartans were given a shield when they were sent out to war, with the admonition to "return in honor behind it, or be carried back on it," but never to yield. So it is with the chan sheng. The agent is given this tool to perform a specific mission. He is trained in its use and instructed how to silence himself and the enemy so that others are not betrayed should he fail. Likewise, the many other uses of the short rope are usually explored in training.

There are many methods of attacking the enemy from behind with the chan sheng. They all rely on a silent approach and a way of dropping the line around the enemy's neck before he can escape or block. In such an attack the rope serves to literally hang the enemy. This is because pressure from the ever-tightening loop acts not only against the windpipe to cut off the air supply and crush the larynx, but also against the carotid artery to stop the flow of blood to the brain. The combination of these actions increases the effectiveness of the technique and renders the enemy unconscious very quickly. Furthermore, the garrote provides an excellent grip on the enemy which enables him to be pulled out of sight with minimal difficulty.

Once the attack begins, the enemy should be brought under control within three seconds. Depending on the individual, unconsciousness will result in thirty seconds to two minutes. The determining factors are the size of the enemy's neck muscles and his lung capacity. Also to be taken into consideration is the fact that a tight cord is not as effective a strangling tool as a soft strip of coiled cloth (obi-jitsu), and that the line will almost certainly inflict some injury upon the throat which will cause the enemy to struggle

violently for as long as he can. Therefore, the enemy must be taken down as quickly as possible to muffle any noise and finished off immediately.

Hadake Jime:
Rear Naked Choke

The most basic attack from behind is also the simplest. Wrap one turn of the line around each fist so that one foot is exposed between them, and follow the steps below.

Sneak up behind the enemy with your hands above his head.

Drop the line over his head as you use your forearms to strike down on his shoulders (top left).

Snatch both fists up and back, drawing the cord taut beneath his chin (center left). Lock your hold by pressing against his back with your elbows.

Step back with the rear foot to break the enemy's balance. Continue to choke him as you drag him out of sight (bottom left). To take him down quickly, drive the right knee forcefully into the base of his spine. This will lift him off his feet, enabling you to drop him straight down. Once he is seated, maintain your hold by pressing your knee between his shoulder blades.

Juji Jime:
Rear Cross Strangle

Unlike many other techniques, the garrote requires that the agent remain in close proximity to the enemy until his enemy is dead. One way to determine whether he is dead is to maintain crushing pressure until the enemy has been completely still for thirty seconds, or by various other means.

Begin with ten inches of the line exposed between the fists and the arms loosely crossed at the forearms (below).

Approach the enemy from behind (below).

Slip the loop over the enemy's head (top right) before he can pull away or raise a defense.

Pull both fists down and back, separating the forearms and directing the cord horizontally across your opponent's larynx (center right).

Cross the line at the base of his skull to draw the loop tight and exert force against his neck (bottom right).

Step back from the enemy, and pull him down at arm's length in order to drag him out of sight.

Mawashi Jime:
Encircling Choke

This is by far the most difficult of the three techniques shown to execute. The chance that the enemy can block the cord by bringing his hand up is great. However, once the line is in place, the enemy is quickly overcome and easily carried away.

The only effective block against any of these attacks is the old judo palm-on-face block. As the garrote drops over the head, it is instinctive for a person to try to grab the cord to prevent being choked. Since the cord cannot be seen, and once in place can hardly be pulled away, this natural reaction is useless. The only hope is to place the hand next to the face, inside the loop before it can be yanked taut. This stalls the attack long enough to formulate a counterstrike.

Wrap one turn round the right wrist, and hold the other end to expose twenty inches of line. Approach your victim from behind.

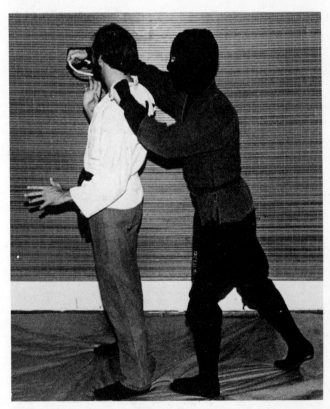

Place your left hand on his left shoulder to distract him as you wrap the line around him from the right side.

Take the slack out of the loop over the enemy's head by pulling your right fist over the left hand.

Turn your right shoulder to rest against his back between his shoulder blades and pull as if lifting a sack onto your shoulder. In this way, the enemy can be quickly carried off.

Fu Ch'ou Ti:
Binding the Enemy

In any endeavor, it is always wise to know the ropes.

Harry Houdini

The next use for a length of cord is to bind the enemy. Although many techniques exist, the following has been employed for centuries without significant change.

The principle is simplicity itself. Begin by tying the left wrist firmly. Thread the free end of the line around the right elbow from behind and then back under itself to form a sliding loop above the joint. Stretch the rope across the back and around the neck, then around the left elbow and over itself to form a second sliding knot above that elbow. Now tie the right wrist securely. If the enemy is seated, any remaining line may be interlaced around the ankles. Then the enemy may be left sitting on his heels as shown, or laid on his stomach. The sliding knot arrangement ensures that any attempt to work free will tighten the loop around the neck and strangle the prisoner, particularly when he is left facedown.

Additional incentive to lie quietly is added by taking up the slack around the diamond-shaped pattern. This raises the fists up between the shoulder blades and quickly numbs the arms. To further secure the enemy, for transport to interrogation for instance, a staff is slid between his elbows and back and the wrists are tied to the center of the belt.

No method of securing a man with rope is designed to be permanent and frequent checks are recommended. Any bonds can be slipped out of, given enough time. The secret of a successful escape is never to really be bound at all. In any escape and evasion, the quicker the attempt is made, the more likely it is to succeed.

Secret Ceremonies 8

A bow is a salutation of courtesy which is rendered to individuals of equal, lesser, or greater rank. In military circles it is taught that the salute originated from knights lifting their visors when in armor to reveal their identities and show that they held no weapon in their right hands. In the martial arts, bowing is an expression of respect for one's sensei or partners. It is performed before and after exercises and kumite (sparring). These are forms of contest in which we express our state of mind. We contend for perfection of technique in practicing, so contestants must respect each other. There are three forms of bow required at the genin level of ninjitsu.

Etiquette requires that one bow when entering the dojo, as a sign of respect for the teachers; and to the judges at a contest. The junior member always bows first. The deeper the bow, the greater the respect which is demonstrated. If the senior belt does not return the bow, it means that he does not recognize you; any further attempt at communication would be considered a challenge. Sometimes the senior belt will bow first. If the student does not respond to the senior belt, it is considered an insult and a challenge. The proper response would be to bow lower than the sensei.

From the position of attention, the feet are loosely placed together at the sides. Fingers are curled, the head is up, and the back is straight. Eyes face forward. Keep your legs straight, but the knees should not be locked. Bend from the waist to an angle of 15 degrees from the vertical position. Keep your eyes on the person to whom the bow is directed.

The salutation presented above is a standard bow, suitable for a greeting between two equals. Note that the eyes remain directed toward the object of the bow. In competition, this is to ensure that the opponent does not launch an unsuspected attack; in salutation, it is to observe that the courtesy is returned.

Kneeling

There are times during a briefing, or when pausing before the next advance, when the attention and at-ease positions are inappropriate. On such occasions, kneeling may be employed.

At the command "Kneel" or "Ready, kneel," or when given the hand sign to duck under cover in the field, drop silently and swiftly downward, bending the left knee and resting on the right and placing your hands on your knees.

In this position, you distort your silhouette, but maintain a position of readiness from which you may quickly spring to your feet to fight or flee.

Sitting

When meditating, eating, resting, or working on a project, one often finds that sitting with the legs crossed tailor fashion is convenient and comfortable.

This would also be the position taken when one is issued the command "Be seated" in class.

Rites of Initiation

During training, many strange and unusual things will be seen and heard. During that time, the sensei will make known to the student his "secret place." This is a site selected by the initiate with the guidance of the instructor. At one point in the ceremony, the applicants are directed to go to this place to receive a sign which will direct their course thereafter. It may be a meteor, flashing across the sky, or in the case of the special agent, secret instructions regarding his part in the mission (these are always given, even if a general briefing is also held). It may seem to be nothing at all. In that event, the participant has an opportunity to discover the "hidden sign" during the next phase. Each sign is significant only to the individual observer, for it represents a part of himself.

The ceremony begins with the applicants being led, blindfolded, to the hidden camp (ni ying ti). All of the members are hooded as the blindfolds are removed. The applicants may be tested or asked questions by the ranking members. Finally they are asked if they would become brothers of the silent way.

A small fire or candle is lit. The members sit on one side and the applicants on the other. Each initiate brings a slip of paper bearing his true name to the gathering. At a sign from the jonin (headman), they recite the following:

"From this day forward, I shall strive for perfection of character; foster the spirit of effort; defend the paths of truth; honor the principles of etiquette; and guard against impetuous courage. I swear never to reveal the secret teachings of the silent way and make this sign of my allegiance . . ." (The jonin passes a small knife or lancet to each man, who pricks a finger and places a drop of blood on the paper bearing his name.) "From this day forth I shall be a brother of the night. May I be destroyed as this paper is consumed [the initiate holds the paper bearing his name and the drop of blood over the fire or candle, letting the flame ignite the paper between his cupped hands] should I ever betray the trust which has been placed in me . . ."

The jonin speaks: "Go now to your secret places; remain there until dawn. When you return tell no one what you have seen or heard."

The fire is extinguished.

At dawn the initiates return to the site of the ritual fire. They sit as before, but now they sit alone. One of the members approaches. He seats himself before the group and bows. This is the Grand Mute.

He is totally disguised so that not even the other members know who he is. In the field, this is the individual to whom all reports are made. Normally he does not speak, but at this time, the new members are allowed to ask any question they desire. They are governed by the principle that if one strikes a gong with a pebble, one receives a small reply; but if one strikes properly with a mallet, one receives the response which is truly desired.

The Grand Mute remains until the meeting is adjourned. He then exits. The adepts now wait for the return of the jonin. He leads them to the rest of the group and reports as follows:

"Behold, those who have left us are no more. They departed as students and return as teachers; they have dropped their self-importance that they may be one with all things. Let us now regard them as brothers, with their gain as our own gain and their loss as our own loss. Let us comfort them in time of sorrow and rejoice with them in victory. For they are Ninja, men of knowledge, and worthy of our respect."

At this time, the adept is presented with a hood or scarf (depending on the ryu), and a weapon (usually a garrote), together with instructions for the use of each.

The garrote is a symbol of the French Croix de Guerre, or rope of war, and indicates that the initiate has participated in a silent mission.

Commentary

The secret initiation ceremony is revealed here so that unsuspecting potential initiates will not be required to submit to the indignities often found in other fraternities. The ingredients are simple: a pledge from one man to another; a promise of help; a symbolic joining of the spirit in a quest that is mutually desirous.

Initiation was an ancient rite when the Sumerians first used it, and although it has undergone many changes over the centuries, and been spoken in many tongues and many lands, it remains nothing more than one individual giving his word to another. This is trust, and if you do not have it, and are not worthy of it, you will never understand the concept of brotherhood, much less participate in any of its rituals.

One of the things that sets Ninja apart from other men is their lack of need for companionship. They are seldom leaders or joiners, being content in the knowledge that each of us must make our own mistakes and our own way in the world. The Ninja seldom give advice, though they are eminently qualified to do so, because they know that those who need it don't listen and those who don't need it already know. The wise man learns from his mistakes; the sage learns from the mistakes of others.

It is not pride that makes the Ninja silent, keeping the knowledge of his adventures and exploits from the prying eyes of others. It is humility and wonderment that he even managed to survive.

Life is sometimes called the Great Game, whose motives are survival and conquest. When mankind is not engaged in one, it is usually engaged in the other. The Ninja survive well, and occasionally participate in the survival or conquests of others.

Exercise of Stillness

Once the body is prepared, the mind must be made ready. This is accomplished by meditation, or, as it is sometimes known, the exercise of stillness.

Sit on a cushion or thick rug which is comfortable for you. Sit in the lotus position if possible; otherwise, sit in the half-lotus or cross the legs Indian style. Always strive to discover the most comfortable and natural position for the body. Relax your shoulders, straighten your back, do not lean, never strain.

Concentrate on the goal of meditation.
Do not listen with your ear but listen with
   your mind;
Not with your mind but with your breath.
Let hearing stop with the ear,
Let the mind stop with its images.
Breathing means to empty oneself and to
   wait for Tao.
Tao abides only in the emptiness.
This emptiness is the fasting mind . . .
Look at the void! In its chamber light
   is produced.
Lo! Joy is here to stay.

                 Chuang Tzu

Postscript

Finally, we would say to the reader: a way is herein shown by which you may pass from darkness into light. This book, however imperfectly, indicates the stages of that way and is the result of our personal experience. We testify to that which we have seen, and we speak that which we do know. That this may also be true for at least some of those who read herein is our sincere wish.

A great deal of ninjitsu is deception. In combat, deceiving the enemy about the gap between your two positions plays a large part in the confrontation. This is accomplished for the most part by the "black-on-black" silhouette presented by the costume. It is possible to move as much as ten inches toward or away from the enemy simply by slowly advancing or withdrawing the hips (hara) over the center of balance. Also, you can quickly bend the knees, so that it appears you are advancing. Both of these techniques may be used to make the enemy misjudge his target.